Grammar Troublespots

An Editing Guide for ESL Students

D1504098

Grammar Troublespots

An Editing Guide for ESL Students

ANN RAIMES

Hunter College,
The City University of New York

St. Martin's Press
New York

Executive Editor: Susan Anker
Project Editor: Beverly Hinton
Text Design: Leon Bolognese
Cover Design: Darby Downey

Library of Congress Catalog Card Number: 87-043104
Copyright © 1988 by St. Martin's Press, Inc.
All rights reserved.
Manufactured in the United States of America.
21098
fedcba

For information, write
St. Martin's Press, Inc.
175 Fifth Avenue
New York, NY 10010

ISBN: 0-312-01602-6

Acknowledgments

p. 86: *Peanuts* cartoon. Copyright © 1959. Courtesy of United Feature Syndicate, Inc.

Preface: To the Instructor

Grammar Troublespots: An Editing Guide for ESL Students offers a modified version of the grammar editing section that is included in *Exploring Through Writing: A Process Approach to ESL Composition* (St. Martin's Press, 1987). There it was part of a whole course built around readings, pictures, and guided instruction through the writing process. Here it is designed either to be used independently by intermediate-advanced ESL students as they edit their college writing assignments, or to accompany whatever course material a writing instructor selects. This book then functions as an editing guide, presenting ways of looking at and critically examining any piece of writing in order to edit it for standard grammar and syntax.

In a writing course, it is recommended that students work through a few sections in class, perhaps *Troublespots 1, 8,* and *9,* either as a whole-class or group activity, each time using authentic pieces of student writing from that class to examine and edit. In this way, as teachers and students ask questions about the sentences on the page in front of them, students see models for the process of examining their own work and applying grammatical principles. Grammatical vocabulary is introduced for editing purposes, but is kept simple; for example, *subject, predicate, noun, verb, article, clause, singular* and *plural* are clear, key concepts for editing purposes. Once students have used several flowcharts and have become familiar with the limited grammatical terminology used in the book, they are able to use the rest of the book independently or as they are referred to specific chapters by their instructor.

ANN RAIMES

Contents

Introduction

Grammar Troublespots offers you help with some important "grammar troublespots" of English that might cause you difficulties in your writing. It is not intended to be a complete review of English grammar, nor is it intended to cover everything you need to know to correct all errors in a piece of writing. Rather, the book concentrates on rules, not exceptions, so it will help you apply general principles. It will also aid you in finding ways to examine and evaluate your own writing in terms of grammatical accuracy.

In *Grammar Troublespots* you will discover explanations for some conventions of standard written English—areas of the language that operate systematically, according to rules. These explanations are accompanied by exercises (an *Answer Key* is included at the back of the book) and by flowcharts that give you specific questions to ask as you evaluate your own writing. By focusing your attention directly on the problem area, these questions will help you find and correct your own errors, either independently or with the help of an instructor. Sometimes, such focusing is precisely what a writer needs in order to find—and correct—errors.

The editing advice given frequently suggests that you seek help: from a classmate, from your instructor, or from a dictionary. Certainly a dictionary such as *Oxford Student's Dictionary of American English* (Oxford University Press, 1983) or *The American Heritage Dictionary of the English Language: New College Edition* (Houghton Mifflin, 1982) is an invaluable tool for checking not only spelling but also irregular plural forms, verb forms, and idioms. Experienced writers often seek advice, so make sure to use the resources around you.

Throughout this book, a sentence preceded by an asterisk (*) indicates an *example sentence* that is not acceptable in standard edited English.

Grammar Troublespots

An Editing Guide for ESL Students

Sentence Structure and Boundaries

> *Question:* **What makes up a sentence, and where does a sentence begin and end?**

A. Which of the following are standard sentences in written English? Which are not?

1. the sun came out.
2. When the sun came out, we all went to the beach.
3. The beach looked lovely
4. The waves splashing on the sand.
5. We playing games.
6. Ate our picnic.
7. Ham sandwiches ate we.
8. We stayed there for four hours, sunbathing and swimming.
9. Because we were having such a good time.

List how these sentences should be written. You can correct the grammar or punctuation, or combine one sentence with the sentence that comes before or after it. (See Answer Key, p. 101.) When you have finished, list what you consider the requirements of a sentence to be.

B. Each of the following examples contains one group of words that is *not* a sentence, even though it has a capital letter and end punctuation. It is only part of a sentence (that is, a *sentence fragment*).

1. The little girl saw a spider. A great big black one.
2. She screamed loudly. To try to scare the spider.
3. Because she was frightened. She ran into another room.
4. She sat down next to her mother. Her legs still shaking.

Determine which is the fragment, and why, according to the list of sentence

requirements you made in Item A. Decide how you could turn the sentence fragment into a complete sentence or include it in another sentence. Write your new
sentences. (See Answer Key, p. 101.)

C. Sentences can be long or short, simple or complex. This is a simple sentence:

The man bought a new car.

It contains one independent clause (a sentence that makes sense alone and can
stand alone). This independent clause has a verb, *bought*, and a subject for the
verb, the person who did the buying, *the man*. In addition, it has an object, telling
us what the man bought—*a new car*. However, we can add other information, too,
and the sentence will still have only one independent clause. It will just be a longer
sentence. We can add information at several points within the sentence, and that
information can take the form of different grammatical structures:

1. *Add information at the beginning.*
   Last week, the man bought a new car.
   Because he felt adventurous, the man bought a new car.
   Although his wife hated the idea, the man bought a new car.
   Wanting to look prosperous, the man bought a new car.
   Bored with his life in the city, the man bought a new car.
   To try to impress his friends, the man bought a new car.

2. *Expand the subject.*
   The rich man bought a new car.
   The man who got a raise last week bought a new car.
   The man who works in my office bought a new car.
   The man working in my office bought a new car.
   The man and his wife bought a new car.
   The man with an old Cadillac bought a new car.

3. *Insert some additional information in the middle.*
   The man in my office, Joseph Moran, bought a new car.
   The man, wanting to impress his friends, bought a new car.
   The man, proud and excited about his raise in salary, bought a new car.

4. *Expand the verb.*
   The man bought and sold a new car.
   The man bought a new car and sold it.

5. *Expand the object.*
   The man bought a fancy new red car.
   The man bought a new car and a computer.

The man bought his wife a new car.
The man bought a new car for his wife.

6. *Add information at the end.*
   The man bought a new car last week.
   The man bought a new car because he felt adventurous.
   The man bought a new car when he could afford it.
   The man bought a new car to try to impress his friends.
   The man bought a new car even though his wife didn't approve.

Note that in each of the preceding sentences, there is only one clause (a subject and verb combination) that can stand alone—the independent clause.

D. Try to expand the following sentence by adding information in different places. See how many different variations you can invent. Refer to Item C for examples of structures that you might add.

The doctor prescribed some pills.

E. Compare your list of the requirements of a sentence (Item A) to the requirements shown in the box below. How many of these requirements did you write down in your list in Item A?

REQUIREMENTS OF A SENTENCE

– A sentence needs a capital letter at the beginning.
– A sentence needs a period, a question mark, or an exclamation point at the end.
– A sentence needs a subject.
– A sentence needs a finite verb (a complete verb phrase—that is, the auxiliaries, such as *is, were, has, had, will, can, might, should have,* and *will be*—along with the verb forms used to form the verb phrase). See Troublespot 8, "Verb Forms."
– A sentence needs standard word order. In English, the regular sequence is SVO (Subject-Verb-Object), with insertions possible at several points in the sequence.
– A sentence needs an independent "core" idea, which can stand alone. This is known as a *main clause* or, as we call it in this book, an *independent clause.*

Editing Advice

Use the following flowchart with a piece of your writing to examine any sentences that you think might have a problem in structure. Begin with the last sentence of your draft and work backward. In this way, you can isolate each sentence from its context and examine it more objectively. Ask these questions for each problematic sentence:

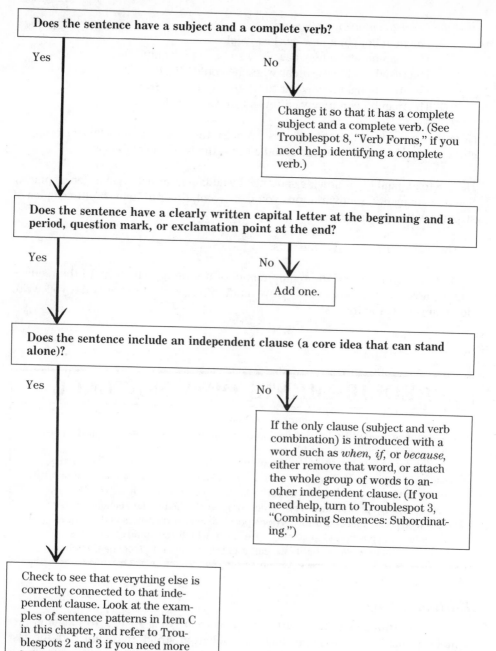

Does the sentence have a subject and a complete verb?

Yes   No

Change it so that it has a complete subject and a complete verb. (See Troublespot 8, "Verb Forms," if you need help identifying a complete verb.)

Does the sentence have a clearly written capital letter at the beginning and a period, question mark, or exclamation point at the end?

Yes   No

Add one.

Does the sentence include an independent clause (a core idea that can stand alone)?

Yes   No

If the only clause (subject and verb combination) is introduced with a word such as *when*, *if*, or *because*, either remove that word, or attach the whole group of words to another independent clause. (If you need help, turn to Troublespot 3, "Combining Sentences: Subordinating.")

Check to see that everything else is correctly connected to that independent clause. Look at the examples of sentence patterns in Item C in this chapter, and refer to Troublespots 2 and 3 if you need more help with combining sentences.

Combining Sentences: Coordinating

Questions: **How do I connect one sentence to another? What options do I have to connect (coordinate) sentences to make the ideas equally important?**

A. You can connect complete sentences together to form a coordinate sentence that will contain two or more independent clauses of equal importance (that is, core ideas). There are several ways to do the following:

$$\mathbf{S + V} \qquad \mathbf{S + V}$$
(subject + verb) + (subject + verb)

Which way you choose will depend on what seems to fit best the content and context of your piece of writing. So, consider all the options, in context, before you choose.

1. When sentences are closely connected and their structure is similar, you can connect them by using a semicolon:

   The man bought a new car; he gave it to his wife as a surprise birthday present.
   My mother took care of the housework; my father earned the money.

2. You can also indicate *how* two independent clauses are related in meaning within a sentence if you coordinate the two clauses by using a comma followed by one of these seven *connecting words:*

$$\mathbf{S + V,} \quad \left\{ \begin{array}{l} \text{and} \\ \text{but} \\ \text{or} \\ \text{nor} \\ \text{so} \\ \text{for} \\ \text{yet} \end{array} \right\} \quad \mathbf{S + V}$$

Examples:

My father earned the money, *and* my uncle paid the rent on the house.

The man bought a new car, *but* his wife didn't know about it.

Important: To connect two independent clauses, a comma is not enough. You need a comma and a connecting word, or you need a semicolon. The following sentences are *not* acceptable English (the asterisk indicates an ungrammatical sentence):

*The man bought a new car his wife didn't know about it. (There is no connecting word between these two independent clauses, nor is there any punctuation to separate them. This is called a *run-on sentence.*)

*The man bought a new car, his wife didn't know about it. (The two clauses are separated only by a comma, yet a period or semicolon is needed. This is called a *comma splice.*)

B. Two independent clauses with the same subject can be condensed into one sentence:

The man bought a new car.
The man changed his job.

These can be condensed as follows:

The man bought a new car and changed his job. (No comma separates the two verbs when they have the same subject.)

C. There are also many *linking expressions* that help to point out how sentences are joined according to meaning. Even if you use one of these words, you still need to separate your sentences with a period or with a semicolon at the end of your first independent clause. For example:

The little girl had always hated spiders. *In fact,* she was absolutely terrified of them.

or   The little girl had always hated spiders; *in fact,* she was absolutely terrified of them.

or   The little girl had always hated spiders. She was, *in fact,* absolutely terrified of them.

or   The little girl had always hated spiders. She was absolutely terrified of them, *in fact.*

Linking words and phrases are set off from the rest of the sentence by commas. A list of some of the most frequently used linking expressions is shown in the box below. The expressions are not necessarily interchangeable. The context determines which is appropriate. If you want to use a linking expression but are not sure which one to use, ask your instructor.

D. Look at the passage beginning: "We can see how children . . . " that appears in Troublespot 18, Item C, p. 81. Make a list of the linking expressions used there. Use the following box to help you. Then, next to each one, write down what the writer's purpose was in using that expression. (See Answer Key, p. 102.)

E. Connect the following pairs of sentences by using punctuation, connecting words, or linking expressions. Remember, you need to determine the relationship between the two sentences before you can choose a connecting word or a linking expression. Write down your new, combined sentences.

1. Hemingway had some individual peculiarities as a writer.
   He always wrote standing up.

2. Hemingway was a gifted journalist, novelist, and short-story writer.
   He was an active sportsman.

3. Hemingway mostly did his writing in pencil on onionskin typewriter paper.
   He turned to his typewriter when the writing was easy for him, such as writing dialogue.

4. Hemingway's room looked untidy at first glance.
   He was a neat person at heart.

LINKING EXPRESSIONS

Writer's purpose	Linking words and phrases
To add an idea:	in addition, furthermore, moreover, also
To show time or sequence:	meanwhile, first, second, then, next, later, finally
To contrast:	however, nevertheless, though, in contrast, on the other hand
To show result:	therefore, thus, consequently, as a result
To emphasize:	in fact, of course, indeed, certainly
To provide an example:	for example, for instance
To generalize or summarize:	in general, overall, in short

5. Hemingway was a sentimental man, keeping his possessions all around him.
   He hardly ever threw anything away.

6. Hemingway always did a surprising amount of rewriting of his novels.
   He wrote the ending to *A Farewell to Arms* thirty-nine times.

7. Hemingway wrote his short story "The Killers" in one morning.
   After lunch, he wrote "Today Is Friday" and "Ten Indians."

8. Hemingway often wrote all through the afternoon and evening without stopping.
   His landlady worried that he wasn't eating enough.

(See Answer Key, p. 102.)

F. The following passage contains some sentences that are not correctly connected and others that would benefit from the addition of a linking expression. Rewrite the passage, avoiding faulty sentence structure and combining sentences by using connecting words or linking expressions.

My grandfather could speak three languages well. He grew up in Poland during the German occupation. His parents took him to the United States in 1946, the family spoke Polish at home most of the time, but my great-grandparents also spoke German because they wanted my grandfather to remain bilingual. Now my grandfather no longer speaks Polish or German at home, he speaks only English. His children don't speak Polish at all. They understand it a little.

(See Answer Key, p. 102.)

Editing Advice

If you feel unsure about how a sentence you have written is connected to the ideas surrounding it, ask yourself these questions:

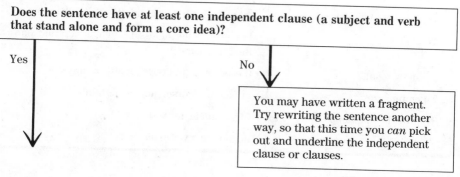

Does the sentence have at least one independent clause (a subject and verb that stand alone and form a core idea)?

Yes

No

You may have written a fragment. Try rewriting the sentence another way, so that this time you *can* pick out and underline the independent clause or clauses.

(Flowchart continued)

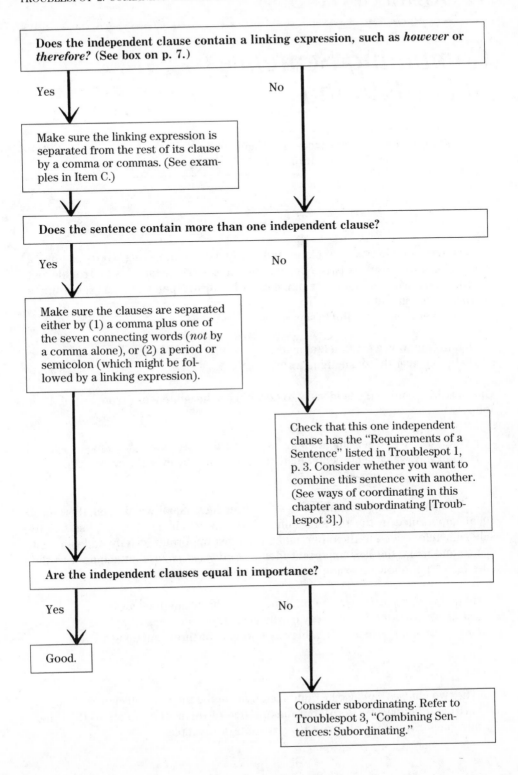

Does the independent clause contain a linking expression, such as *however* or *therefore*? (See box on p. 7.)

Yes   No

Make sure the linking expression is separated from the rest of its clause by a comma or commas. (See examples in Item C.)

Does the sentence contain more than one independent clause?

Yes   No

Make sure the clauses are separated either by (1) a comma plus one of the seven connecting words (*not* by a comma alone), or (2) a period or semicolon (which might be followed by a linking expression).

Check that this one independent clause has the "Requirements of a Sentence" listed in Troublespot 1, p. 3. Consider whether you want to combine this sentence with another. (See ways of coordinating in this chapter and subordinating [Troublespot 3].)

Are the independent clauses equal in importance?

Yes   No

Good.

Consider subordinating. Refer to Troublespot 3, "Combining Sentences: Subordinating."

TROUBLESPOT 3

Combining Sentences: Subordinating

> **Question:** How are sentences put together to make one idea subordinate to another?

A. You can combine two simple sentences by using connecting words or linking expressions; the result is two independent clauses (see examples in Troublespot 2). You also have the option of making one of your independent ideas subordinate to, that is, dependent on, the other.

Look at these two simple sentences:

Hemingway was a sentimental man.
He hardly ever threw anything away.

One way to combine these ideas is to coordinate the sentences (Troublespot 2) as follows:

Hemingway was a sentimental man, so he hardly ever threw anything away.
Hemingway was a sentimental man. In fact, he hardly ever threw anything away.

In the preceding example, the two clauses have equal weight and, therefore, equal importance in the reader's mind. One way to change the emphasis is to subordinate one idea to the other: make the most important idea the independent clause and make the less important idea a *condensed phrase*, attaching it to the core idea. The following examples include condensed phrases:

Hemingway, *a sentimental man*, hardly ever threw anything away.
Being sentimental, Hemingway hardly ever threw anything away.
For sentimental reasons, Hemingway hardly ever threw anything away.

B. The two clauses can also be combined by keeping them as full clauses (subject + verb) and (subject + verb), but making one of them subordinate to the other by introducing it with a *subordinating word*. For example:

Hemingway, *who was a sentimental man,* hardly ever threw anything away.
Because Hemingway was a sentimental man, he hardly ever threw anything away.

The dependent clause of each of these two sentences is in italics. Note that it
cannot stand alone. It has been made subordinate to the independent clause and
is now dependent on it for meaning. The following is not a complete sentence but
a *fragment:*

*Because Hemingway was a sentimental man.

C. The accompanying box shows both the relationships that allow one sentence
to be subordinated to another (type of clause) and the subordinating words used
to begin dependent clauses.

DEPENDENT CLAUSES

Type of clause	*Examples of subordinating words*
Relative	that, who, whom, which, whose (*that, whom, which* are some-times omitted as the object of the clause) The man *who* won the lottery bought a new car. The man [that] I met last night is an accountant.
Time	when, before, after, until, since, as soon as *When* he won the money, he decided to buy a car.
Place	where, wherever She drove *wherever* she wanted.
Cause	because, as, since She got a parking ticket *because* she parked illegally.
Purpose	so that, in order that He drove fast *so that* he could get to work on time.
Result	so . . . that, such . . . that He drove *so* fast *that* he got a speeding ticket.
Condition	if, unless *If* she hadn't won the lottery, she would have been very unhappy.
Concession	although, even though *Although* she thought she was a good driver, she got a lot of tickets for speeding.
Included statement *or* question	that (sometimes omitted), what, why, how, where, when, who, whom, which, whose, whether, if He knows *why* he gets so many tickets. He knows [that] his business will be successful.

D. Short sentences can thus be combined to make longer sentences by coordinating clauses, subordinating clauses, or by condensing core ideas into phrases. Combine the following short independent clauses into longer sentences by using coordinating or subordinating words, or by condensing ideas. Find as many ways as you can to rewrite these sentences.

Jack wanted to make a good impression.
Jack wore a suit.
The suit was new.
The suit belonged to his brother.
Jack was our administrative assistant.
The suit was big for him.
The pants kept falling down.

(See Answer Key, p. 102.)

E. Read the way one student found to combine these seven sentences into one:

Wanting to make a good impression, Jack, our administrative assistant, wore his brother's new suit, but the suit was so big for him that the pants kept falling down.

Examine the structure of this new sentence by answering these questions:

1. How many independent clauses are there? What are they?
2. What is the subject and verb of each independent clause?
3. If there is more than one independent clause, how are the independent clauses connected?
4. How many subordinate clauses (a subject + verb combination preceded by a subordinating word) are there?
5. How have other core ideas been attached to the independent clause(s)?

(See Answer Key, p. 103.)

Examine the structure of some of the new sentences you formed by asking the same questions.

F. In a similar way, long sentences can be broken down into their short, core parts. This breakdown is a useful way for you to check the structure of any long sentences you write. The following long sentence is from *Minor Characters* by Joyce Johnson:

Her picture as a young woman, placed on the polished lid [of the piano] that's never opened except when the piano tuner comes, is in a heavy silver frame of ornate primitive design brought by my uncle from Peru.

To examine which ideas Johnson combined and how she combined them, separate the sentence into short sentences (like the ones in Item D). That is, break the sentence down into its basic set of core ideas (expressed in a series of independent clauses), so that all the ideas in the sentence are included. Begin like this:

Her picture is in a heavy silver frame.

(See Answer Key, p. 103.)

G. Find as many ways as you can to combine each of the following sentence groups into one sentence. Include all the ideas that are there, but collapse sentences into words or phrases, if you want. You can also add words (subordinating words, for example, or connecting words like *and* and *but*) that will help you to combine the ideas. Use the chart of subordinating words in Item C to help you, too.

1. I watched a little girl.
   She was carrying a big shopping bag.
   I felt sorry for her.
   I offered to help.

2. My family was huge.
   My family met at my grandparents' house every holiday.
   There were never enough chairs.
   I always had to sit on the floor.

3. Computers save time.
   Many businesses are buying them.
   The managers have to train people to operate the machines.
   Sometimes they don't realize that.

4. All their lives they have lived with their father.
   Their father is a politician.
   He is powerful.
   He has made lots of enemies.

5. She wanted to be successful.
   She worked day and night.
   She worked for a famous advertising agency.
   Eventually she became a vice president.

6. He really wants to go skiing.
   He has decided to go to a beach resort in California.
   His sister lives in the beach resort.
   He hasn't seen her for 10 years.

(See Answer Key, p. 103.)

Which sentence of each group did you select as the independent clause of your new sentence? Why did you select that one? How does the meaning of your sentence change if you choose a different independent clause?

Editing Advice

1. If you find any groups of sentences in your writing that seem short and need some variation, ask these questions:

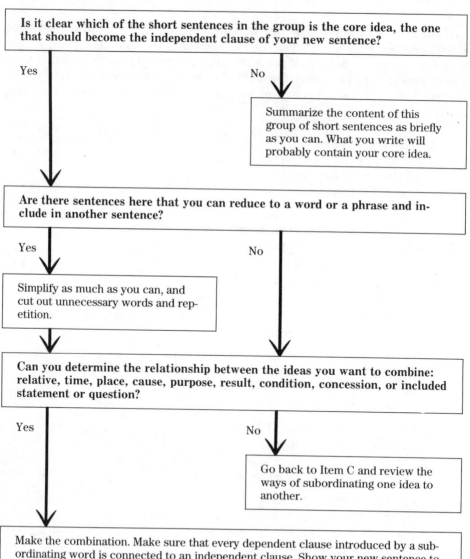

Is it clear which of the short sentences in the group is the core idea, the one that should become the independent clause of your new sentence?

Yes

No

Summarize the content of this group of short sentences as briefly as you can. What you write will probably contain your core idea.

Are there sentences here that you can reduce to a word or a phrase and include in another sentence?

Yes

No

Simplify as much as you can, and cut out unnecessary words and repetition.

Can you determine the relationship between the ideas you want to combine: relative, time, place, cause, purpose, result, condition, concession, or included statement or question?

Yes

No

Go back to Item C and review the ways of subordinating one idea to another.

Make the combination. Make sure that every dependent clause introduced by a subordinating word is connected to an independent clause. Show your new sentence to a classmate or to your instructor to see if they prefer it to the original series of sentences.

2. Now look for sentences that seem a bit too involved and complicated for a reader to figure out. Ask the following:

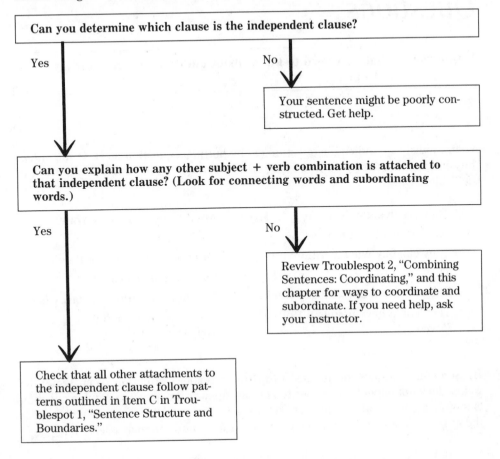

Can you determine which clause is the independent clause?

Yes

No

Your sentence might be poorly constructed. Get help.

Can you explain how any other subject + verb combination is attached to that independent clause? (Look for connecting words and subordinating words.)

Yes

No

Review Troublespot 2, "Combining Sentences: Coordinating," and this chapter for ways to coordinate and subordinate. If you need help, ask your instructor.

Check that all other attachments to the independent clause follow patterns outlined in Item C in Troublespot 1, "Sentence Structure and Boundaries."

TROUBLESPOT 4

Questions

> **Question:** **What do I need to know about questions when I edit my writing?**

A. In English, we indicate a question (1) by putting a question mark at the end of the sentence and (2) by putting an *auxiliary verb* (i.e., a helping verb) in front of the subject.

They are living in New York.	*Are* they living in New York?
They have a lot of money.	*Do* they have a lot of money?
They can buy whatever they want.	*Can* they buy whatever they want?
They like fast cars.	*Do* they like fast cars?
They bought a Porsche last week.	*Did* they buy a Porsche last week?
They could have bought a Rolls-Royce.	*Could* they have bought a Rolls-Royce?

B. Sometimes a question is useful to draw a reader's attention to an issue; the writer does not expect the reader to actually answer the question. Such a question is simply a rhetorical device that lets a reader know that the writer will answer the question. Look at the following examples from books and articles:

But what's happening when we feel overwhelmed, rather than consoled, by too many objects that we nonetheless don't want to part with and continue collecting? (Barbara Lang Stern, "Lure of Possessions")

What did I actually learn from all my summer and after-school jobs? (Susan Allen Toth, *Blooming: A Small-Town Girlhood*)

How can he possibly envision anyone analyzing a system or researching a market? (Russell Baker, "The Paper Workingstuff")

Is this gap responsible for the declining growth rate of the nation's productivity? (Julia Kagan, "Survey: Work in the 1980s and 1990s")

Why don't fringe benefits, lack of stress, and good working conditions produce motivation to work hard? (Julia Kagan, "Survey: Work in the 1980s and 1990s")

Who teaches us this instinct? Where does the habit come from? (Bruce Mays, "In Fighting Trim")

Questions are also used as titles of articles and essays:

Are Women Bosses Better? (Mary Schnack)
What Do Women Really Want? (William Novak)

C. When a question is reported within a statement, it no longer functions as a question. Both the word order and the final punctuation become the same as in a statement.

Direct question: She often asks, "What do I need to do next?"
Reported question: She often asks what she needs to do next.

Direct question: He wants to know, "What did she say?"
Reported question: He wants to know what she said.

See also Troublespot 19, "Reporting and Paraphrasing."

D. Look at the sentences about Hemingway that appear in Troublespot 2, Item E, pp. 7–8. Write ten questions about Hemingway that these sentences could answer. Imagine that you are giving a test to a class of students. Some suggested beginnings follow:

What kind of . . . ?	Was . . . ?
On what kind of . . . ?	Did . . . ?
What . . . ?	Why . . . ?
How much . . . ?	How many times . . . ?
Which story?	Who . . . ?

E. Look at the cartoon in Troublespot 19. Write three questions that *you* would ask Lucy.

Editing Advice

If you have problems forming questions, look at your writing and ask the following questions:

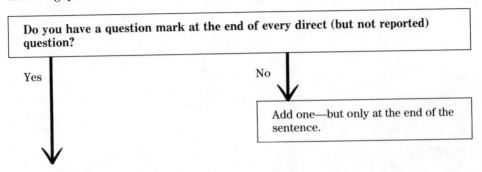

Do you have a question mark at the end of every direct (but not reported) question?

Yes

No

Add one—but only at the end of the sentence.

(Flowchart continued)

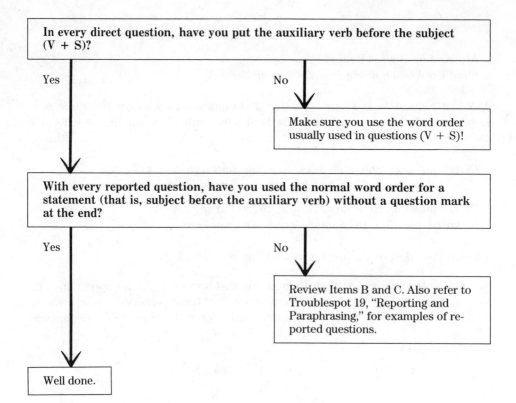

In every direct question, have you put the auxiliary verb before the subject (V + S)?

Yes

No

Make sure you use the word order usually used in questions (V + S)!

With every reported question, have you used the normal word order for a statement (that is, subject before the auxiliary verb) without a question mark at the end?

Yes

No

Review Items B and C. Also refer to Troublespot 19, "Reporting and Paraphrasing," for examples of reported questions.

Well done.

Negatives

> **Question:** What do I have to check when I use a negative in a
> sentence?

A. In some languages, the negative can occur in various positions in a sentence.
In English, the adverb *not* comes after the first verb in the clause.

Sally has *not* been to London.
She is *not* planning to go this year.

B. *Not* can be contracted with some auxiliary verbs. However, contractions are
usually used only in informal writing, such as in letters and journals. Contractions
are generally not used in more formal writing, such as essays or textbooks. (When
you write an essay, ask your instructor if contractions are acceptable.) Examples
of contractions include: *isn't, aren't, wasn't, weren't, doesn't, don't, didn't, hasn't,
haven't,* and *can't.* Note that the contraction for *will not* is *won't.*

C. English uses only *one* negative in a clause. For instance:

She did*n't* do anything.
She did *nothing.*

A double negative is incorrect.

*She did*n't* do *nothing.*

D. Alternative ways of expressing negation are shown in the following lists.

Regular form	*Alternative form*
not a	no
not any	no
not any of	none of
not anyone	no one
not anybody	nobody
not anything	nothing
not anywhere	nowhere
not ever	never
not either	neither

Examples:

Researchers find that workers do*n't* have *any* real incentive.
Researchers find that workers have *no* real incentive.
He ca*n't* justify *any* of his expenditures.
He can justify *none* of his expenditures.
She ca*n't* explain *either* of her decisions.
She can explain *neither* of her decisions.

E. You can give special emphasis to the negative *never* by placing it first in the sentence. In such a case, however, the first auxiliary verb must come *before* the subject.

I *have never* seen such a sloppy piece of work.
Never have I seen such a sloppy piece of work!

The first place in the sentence also provides emphasis for the expression *not only . . . but also.*

The couple *not only took care* of the housework *but also* tended the garden.
Not only did the couple *take care* of the housework, *but* they *also* tended the garden.

Note the word order (and the verb form) when *not only* is placed first in the sentence.

F. *Neither* can be used as a sentence negative. Its meaning is equivalent to *not . . . either*, but it is more emphatic.

The mother doesn't have much free time. The children do*n't either.*
The mother doesn't have much free time, and *neither* do the children.

Note also how *either . . . or* and *neither . . . nor* are used:

The children don't have *either* a full-time mother *or* father at home.
or   The children have *neither* a full-time mother *nor* father at home.

Neither the mother *nor* the children have much free time.
or   *Neither* the children *nor* the mother has much free time.

What is the difference between the verb forms in the last two sentences? What could account for the use of the plural form *(have)* and the singular form *(has)?* (See Answer Key, p. 103.)

G. Rewrite the underlined sections in the following passage, using an alternative way of expressing negation. Refer to the lists in Item D.

"Workaholics" are people who are addicted to work. They <u>don't have any time</u> for their family. They <u>don't think anything</u> is as important as their job and doing well in that job. Workaholics <u>can't ever really relax;</u> they are always tense, anxious, and irritable about finishing a project. They <u>will go nowhere</u> unless they take work along with them. One workaholic has been seen adding columns of figures while trying to sail a boat in a storm! Often, on a weekend away, workaholics <u>will talk to nobody</u>, except, of course, when they call their office, which they usually do a few times a day.

(See Answer Key, p. 104.)

H. Write a paragraph about a sports fan you know or about someone with a passionate hobby or interest. Use some of the structures discussed in this chapter. Underline the negatives you use.

Editing Advice

If you have been having problems with negatives, examine each negative form in your piece of writing and ask the following questions:

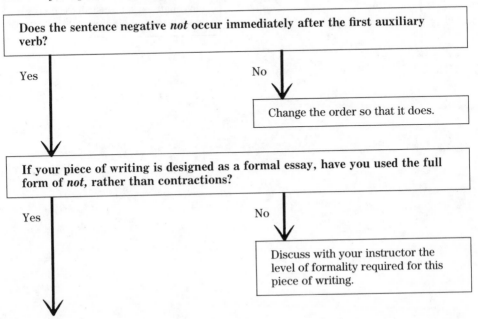

(Flowchart continued)

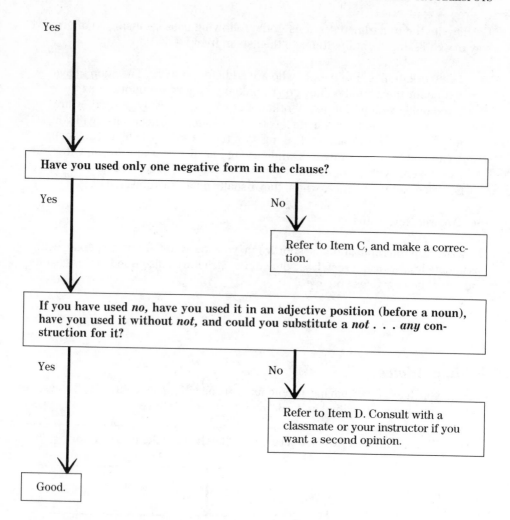

Yes

Have you used only one negative form in the clause?

Yes

No

Refer to Item C, and make a correction.

If you have used *no,* have you used it in an adjective position (before a noun), have you used it without *not,* and could you substitute a *not . . . any* construction for it?

Yes

No

Refer to Item D. Consult with a classmate or your instructor if you want a second opinion.

Good.

Nouns

Question: What do I need to know about nouns to edit my writing?

A. Nouns can be classified as follows:

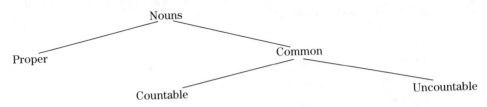

B. The two major classes are *proper* and *common* nouns.

1. Proper nouns include, for instance, names of specific people, countries, cities, rivers, languages, places, buildings, schools, months, and days of the week. They begin with capital letters. (See also Items A and D in Troublespot 12, "Articles.") For example:

   My birthday is in *January.*
   The *River Thames* runs through *London,* past the *Houses of Parliament. Henry Wright* went to *Columbia University* last *September* to study *French.*

2. If a noun is not a proper noun, it is a common noun. For example, names of objects and animals are common nouns. These nouns do not begin with capital letters. In addition, they are often preceded by one or more *determiners,* as listed below:

   - articles: *a, an, the* (See Troublespot 12, "Articles.")
   - demonstrative adjectives: *this, that, these, those* (See Troublespot 11, "Pronouns.")
   - possessive adjectives: *my, his, our,* etc. (See Troublespot 11, "Pronouns.")
   - possessive nouns: *Sally's, the group's,* etc. (See Troublespot 20, "Apostrophes for Possession.")

- quantity words: *some, many, much, a lot of,* etc. (See Item E.)
- numerals: *one, two, seventeen,* etc.

C. *Countable nouns* form one of the two classes of common nouns. Note the following:

1. Countable nouns have a plural form:

   The little *girls* sat down on the grass. They ate some *cookies.*

2. The most common way to form a plural of a countable noun is to add *-s* or *-es.* Add it even when there is a numeral included to tell the reader there is more than one. Note that the ending *-y* changes to *-ies* when *-y* is preceded by a consonant.

one girl	two girls
a box	some boxes
one match	a lot of matches
a party	three parties

   Some words do not use *-s* for the plural. For example:

one man	two men
a child	many children
that tooth	those teeth

   Use your dictionary to check any plurals that you are not sure of.

D. *Uncountable nouns* form the second of the two classes of common nouns. In the context of the sentence we used previously, there is an uncountable noun:

The little girls sat down on the *grass.* They ate some cookies.

Grass is here an uncountable, mass noun, meaning *lawn.* (However, in another context, *grass* can be a countable noun, and its plural is *grasses.*)

   Countable and uncountable nouns vary from language to language. In English, some nouns do not have a plural form because they are considered essentially uncountable: *advice, enjoyment, equipment, furniture, happiness, homework, information, knowledge,* and *luggage.*

Examples:

I asked for some *information.*
He gave me a lot of *information.*

She took a lot of *luggage* on her trip.
She took ten pieces of *luggage* on her trip. (*Luggage* has no plural form;
    pieces indicates the plural.)

There are other mass nouns that can be considered as countable or uncountable, depending on the context:

UNCOUNTABLE: *Chocolate* is fattening. (all chocolate: mass noun)
COUNTABLE: He ate a *chocolate*. (one piece; one serving in a box of chocolates: countable)
Then he ate four more *chocolates*.

E. Note the use of quantity words with nouns. Some quantity words (e.g., *some, a lot of, lots of, no, not any*) can be used with either **countable** plural nouns or **uncountable** nouns. Others (e.g., *many, several, a little*) can be used with only one of the two. Use the accompanying box, "Quantity Words," to help you if you are in doubt.

F. Identify the nouns in the following eight sentences from *Growing Up* by Russell Baker and categorize them as (1) common *(C)* or proper *(P)*; (2) countable

---

QUANTITY WORDS

With uncountable nouns (e.g., luggage, information, happiness)	*With countable plural nouns (e.g., girls, cookies, children, luxuries)*
not much a little (very) little a great deal of less	(not) many a few (very) few several fewer

The following quantity words can be used with both uncountable and plural countable nouns:

some
any
a lot of
lots of
no
not any

(count) or uncountable *(unc);* and (3) if countable, as singular *(s)* or plural *(pl).* Write down the nouns and their identifying abbreviation. For example:

James bought a dozen eggs, some rice, and a melon.

James: P
eggs: C, count, pl.
rice: C, unc.
melon: C, count, s.

1. I was enjoying the luxuries of a rustic nineteenth-century boyhood, but for the women Morrisonville life had few rewards.
2. Both my mother and grandmother kept house very much as women did before the Civil War.
3. They had no electricity, gas, plumbing, or central heating.
4. For baths, laundry, and dishwashing, they hauled buckets of water from a spring at the foot of a hill.
5. They scrubbed floors on hands and knees, thrashed rugs with carpet beaters, killed and plucked their own chickens, baked bread and pastries, patched the family's clothing on treadle-operated sewing machines . . . .
6. By the end of a summer day a Morrisonville woman had toiled like a serf.
7. [The men] scrubbed themselves in enamel basins and, when supper was eaten, climbed up onto Ida Rebecca's porch to watch the night arrive.
8. Presently the women joined them, and the twilight music of Morrisonville began.

(See Answer Key, p. 104.)

G. Decide where the student who wrote the following paragraph made mistakes with noun capitals and plurals. Be careful: *some, any,* and *a lot of* can be used with uncountable as well as countable nouns, as in *a lot of money* and *a lot of books* (see Item E). How would you explain to the student what was done wrong and what must be done to correct the errors?

   When I saw my two ancient suitcase, I knew it was time to buy some new luggage. I looked in the windows of all the store in the center of the Town. But all I saw was clothing. I tried on three dress but didn't buy any. At last, I saw a wonderful leather bag made in spain, but it was too expensive.

(See Answer Key, p. 105.)

Editing Advice

Look at any noun you have written that seems problematic, and ask these questions:

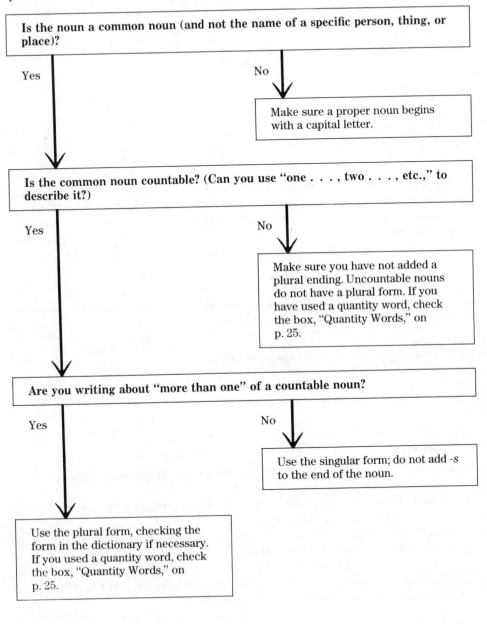

Is the noun a common noun (and not the name of a specific person, thing, or place)?

Yes

No

Make sure a proper noun begins with a capital letter.

Is the common noun countable? (Can you use "one . . . , two . . . , etc.," to describe it?)

Yes

No

Make sure you have not added a plural ending. Uncountable nouns do not have a plural form. If you have used a quantity word, check the box, "Quantity Words," on p. 25.

Are you writing about "more than one" of a countable noun?

Yes

No

Use the singular form; do not add -s to the end of the noun.

Use the plural form, checking the form in the dictionary if necessary. If you used a quantity word, check the box, "Quantity Words," on p. 25.

TROUBLESPOT 7

Verb Tenses

> **Question:** How do I decide which verb tense to use?

A. When you write, there are two main things to consider about verb tense: (1) appropriateness and (2) consistency. First, how do you choose the appropriate verb tense? For the most commonly used active-voice verbs, use the following tables and example sentences to help you establish which of four time relationships you want to express. (For the passive voice, see Troublespot 10.)

Time Relationship Expressed: Simple Time

Past	*Present*	*Future*
She wrote.	She writes.	She will write.
		She is going to write.

Examples:

She *wrote* a story yesterday. (Completed in definite and known past time: e.g., last week, a month ago, in 1984.)

She *writes* every day. (Repeated action or habit in present time: e.g., once a week, whenever she can, often.)

She *will write* a novel next year. (Future time stated or implied: e.g., in the next six months, before she is thirty.)

Note: In clauses beginning with *when, before,* or *as soon as,* use the present and not the future tense for simple time. For example:

When she *arrives,* we'll begin the meeting.

Time Relationship Expressed: In Progress at a Known Time

Past	*Present*	*Future*
She was writing.	She is writing.	She will be writing.

Examples:

She *was writing* when I called her at 8 P.M. last night. (Happening and continuing at a known or stated time in the past: I interrupted her; she probably continued afterward.)

She *was writing* all day yesterday. (Happening continuously over a period of time in the past.)

She *is writing* at this moment. (Happening in the present, right now.)

She *will be writing* when you call her at 8 P.M. tonight. (Happening continuously at a known or stated time in the future: she will probably continue writing after you call.)

Note: The *-ing* form is not used for verbs expressing states of mind (*believe, know, understand, want, hate, seem, need,* etc.); senses (*taste, smell,* etc.); or possession (*have, own,* etc.). The simple forms are used instead.

Time Relationship Expressed: Completed *Before* a Known Time or Event

Past	*Present*	*Future*
she had written	she has written	she will have written

Examples:

She *had* already *written* one story when she started high school. (Two past events are indicated: an activity was completed by a stated time in the past. She wrote the story when she was twelve; she started high school when she was fourteen.)

She *has* (already, just) *written* two stories. (An activity was completed some time before the present. The main point is not *when* she actually wrote them, but that she *has written* them at some time in the past, with the effect being relative to present time.)

She *will* (already) *have written* three stories when she graduates from high school next year. (Two future events are indicated: an activity will be completed by a stated time in the future. First she will write the stories; then she will graduate.)

Time Relationship: In Progress for a Stated Length of Time and up to a Known and Specific Time or Event

Past	*Present*	*Future*
She had been writing.	She has been writing.	She will have been writing.

Examples:

She *had been writing* for three hours before all the lights went out. (One
   event was interrupted by the other; both the length of time and the end
   of the action in the past are usually stated.)
She *has been writing* a novel for two years. (Length of time is stated or
   implied and continues until the present: she will probably continue; she
   has not finished the novel yet. Often used with *for* and *since*.)
She *will have been writing* for six hours by the time the party starts at 8
   P.M. tonight. (An event in the future interrupts or indicates the end of
   the action; both length of time and final event must be stated or clear
   from the context.)

B. Consistency of tenses is important. Usually, the verb tenses a writer uses in a
passage will fit consistently into one of two time zones: (1) Past or (2) Present/
Future. The accompanying box summarizes the four tense/time relationships described in Item A, and divides them into two time zones:

TENSE/TIME RELATIONSHIPS

Time relationship	*Past zone*	*Present/Future zone*	
simple	wrote	writes	will write
in progress	was writing	is writing	will be writing
completed	had written	has written	will have written
in progress for . . . and up to . . .	had been writing	has been writing	will have been writing

Auxiliaries other than *has/had* and *is/was* show the time zone distinction,
too (see Item B in Troublespot 8 for list of auxiliaries):

Past zone	*Present/Future zone*
did	does/do
would	will (would)
could	can (could)
should	shall (should)
might	may (might)
had to	must

C. Do not surprise or confuse your reader by switching from one zone to another in the middle of a paragraph, unless you have a good reason. In the following paragraph, for instance, the time zone switches from Present/Future to Past at the point marked with an asterisk, but the reader is not surprised. Why not? What does the writer do to prepare us for the switch?

I think that big families can offer their members a lot of support. When a child has done something wrong, there is always someone to turn to. Or if a child feels upset about a fight with a friend, even if the child's mother isn't at home, an aunt or a grandmother will be able to comfort him or her and offer advice. *Once when I was six years old, I fell off my bicycle. I had been riding very fast around the block in a race with my friends. My father was working and my mother was out shopping. But the house was still full of people: my aunt bathed my knees, my grandmother gave me a glass of milk and a cookie, and my uncle drove me to the doctor's office.

(See Answer Key, p. 105.)

D. Read the following passage from "Mr. Doherty Builds His Dream Life" by Jim Doherty:

We love the smell of the earth warming and the sound of cattle lowing. We watch for hawks in the sky and deer in the cornfields.

But the good life can get pretty tough. Three months ago when it was 30 below, we spent two miserable days hauling firewood up the river on a toboggan. Three months from now, it will be 95 above and we will be cultivating corn, weeding strawberries and killing chickens. Recently, Sandy and I had to reshingle the back roof. Soon Jim, 16, and Emily, 13, the youngest of our four children, will help me make some long-overdue improvements on the privy that supplements our indoor plumbing when we are working outside. Later this month, we'll spray the orchard, paint the barn, plant the garden and clean the hen house before the new chicks arrive.

Now, underline each complete verb phrase, and identify (1) which time zone (Past, Present, or Future) it fits into, (2) what time is expressed, and (3) what signals, if any, Doherty gives for any switches. Write down the verbs and your identifications. For example: *love:* Present/simple present

(See Answer Key, p. 105.)

E. Choose an article that interests you in a newspaper or magazine. Underline the verbs, and identify what time is expressed according to the boxes in Item B.

Editing Advice

If you are having problems with verb tenses, look at all the active voice verbs in your writing, one paragraph at a time, and ask these questions:

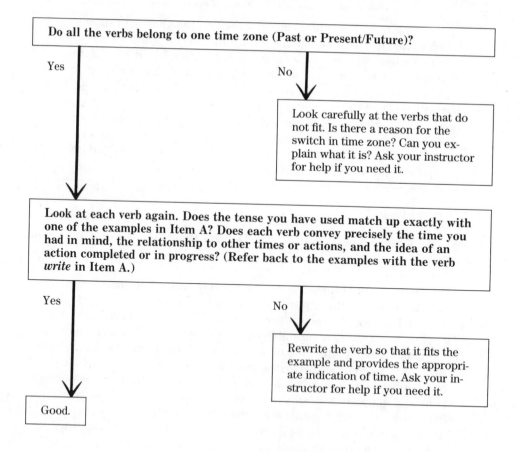

Do all the verbs belong to one time zone (Past or Present/Future)?

Yes

No

Look carefully at the verbs that do not fit. Is there a reason for the switch in time zone? Can you explain what it is? Ask your instructor for help if you need it.

Look at each verb again. Does the tense you have used match up exactly with one of the examples in Item A? Does each verb convey precisely the time you had in mind, the relationship to other times or actions, and the idea of an action completed or in progress? (Refer back to the examples with the verb *write* in Item A.)

Yes

No

Rewrite the verb so that it fits the example and provides the appropriate indication of time. Ask your instructor for help if you need it.

Good.

Verb Forms

Question: How do I know which verb form goes with which auxiliary?

A. Look at these verb forms:

Simple (no -s)	-s	-ing	Past	Participle
paint	paints	painting	painted	painted
sing	sings	singing	sang	sung
take	takes	taking	took	taken

There are regular rules about which verb forms are used with which auxiliary verbs to form a complete (or *finite*) verb in a clause or sentence. There are no exceptions. So, choose which verb form to use according to the helping verb you use. The chart given in Item B will help you determine which verb form to use. Irregular verb forms are listed in the Appendix.

B. In the accompanying chart, note that *only* the shaded forms of the verb are possible after the helping verbs (auxiliaries) listed in the left-hand column.

Verb Forms

I. Verb form used after an auxiliary

Auxiliary(ies)	Simple (no -s)	-s	-ing	Past	Participle
DO does/do did					

(Chart continued)

Auxiliary(ies)	Simple (no *-s*)	*-s*	*-ing*	Past	Participle
WILL will would can could shall should may might must					
HAVE has/have had will have would have can have could have shall have should have may have might have must have					
BE am/is/are was/were has been/ have been had been will be would be can be could be shall be should be may be might be must be will have been would have been can have been					Passive (see p. 42)

Auxiliary(ies)	Simple (no -s)	-s	-ing	Past	Participle
BE (cont.) could have been shall have been should have been may have been might have been must have been					Passive (see p. 42)
BEING am/is/are being was/were being					Passive (see p. 42)

II. Verb form used with no auxiliary

Time	Simple (no -s)	-s	-ing	Past	Participle
Simple time (past)					
Simple time (present) (*he, she, it* forms as subject)					
Simple time (present) (*I, you, we, they* forms as subject)					

You see from the chart that, for most auxiliary sequences, the form of the verb after an auxiliary is fixed. You do not have to guess which form to use. Only with the *be* forms do you have a choice: you need to determine whether you want an active or a passive form before you decide whether to use the *-ing* or the participle form.

C. In the following two passages from articles, underline each complete (finite) verb phrase. As you do so, look at the preceding chart, and note where each verb phrase fits into the chart.

   1. About half of the children whose parents had divorced hadn't seen their father in the last year; only one out of six had managed to see their father an average of once a week. If the current rate of divorce persists, about half of all children will spend some time in a single-parent family before they reach 18.

Much has been written about the psychological effects on children of living with one parent, but the literature has not yet proven that any lasting negative effects occur. One effect, however, does occur with regularity: women who head single-parent families typically experience a sharp decline in their income relative to before their divorce. Husbands usually do not experience a decline. (Cherlin and Furstenberg, "The American Family in the Year 2000")

2. In the common everyday job, nothing is made any more. Things are now made by machines. Very little is repaired. The machines that make things make them in such a fashion that they will quickly fall apart in such a way that repairs will be prohibitively expensive. Thus the buyer is encouraged to throw the thing away and buy a new one. In effect, the machines are making junk. (Russell Baker, "The Paper Workingstuff ")

(See Answer Key, p. 105.)

D. Choose a reading that interests you in a newspaper, a magazine, or a book, and examine each verb as you did in Item C.

Editing Advice

Look at all the complete verbs you have written in a paragraph. Use the Appendix to check irregular verb forms. Ask these questions:

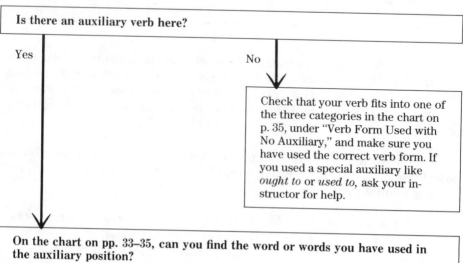

Is there an auxiliary verb here?

Yes   No

Check that your verb fits into one of the three categories in the chart on p. 35, under "Verb Form Used with No Auxiliary," and make sure you have used the correct verb form. If you used a special auxiliary like *ought to* or *used to*, ask your instructor for help.

On the chart on pp. 33–35, can you find the word or words you have used in the auxiliary position?

(Flowchart continued)

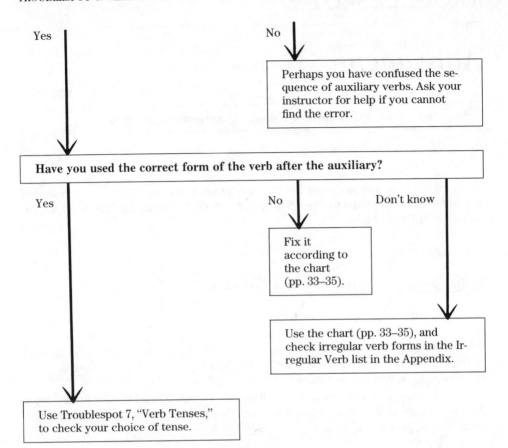

Yes

No

Perhaps you have confused the sequence of auxiliary verbs. Ask your instructor for help if you cannot find the error.

Have you used the correct form of the verb after the auxiliary?

Yes

No

Don't know

Fix it according to the chart (pp. 33–35).

Use the chart (pp. 33–35), and check irregular verb forms in the Irregular Verb list in the Appendix.

Use Troublespot 7, "Verb Tenses," to check your choice of tense.

TROUBLESPOT 9

Agreement

> **Question:** How can I solve problems of agreement in my writing?

A. In a clause or a sentence in the present tense, make sure that the verb agrees in number with its subject—specifically, with the head noun (i.e., the most important noun) of its subject.

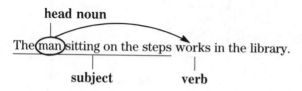

If the head noun is a *he/she/it* form, use the third person singular form (*-s* ending) of the verb. If the head noun is a *they* form, use the plural form of the verb (i.e., the simple form with no *-s* ending).

Determining singular or plural endings can be confusing because an *-s* ending on a noun indicates plural (i.e., *they* form), while an *-s* ending on a verb indicates singular (i.e., *he/she/it*) form.

The dog bark*s* every night. (*Dog* = "it," so the verb is singular.)
The dog*s* bark every night. (*Dogs* = "they," so the verb is plural.)

B. Read the following excerpt from "Mr. Doherty Builds His Dream Life" by Jim Doherty).

> Sandy, meanwhile, pursues her own hectic rounds. Besides the usual household routine, she oversees the garden and beehives, bakes bread, cans and freezes, chauffeurs the kids to their music lessons, practices with them, takes organ lessons on her own, does research and typing for me, writes an article herself now and then, tends the flower beds, stacks a little wood and delivers the eggs.

Underline all the verbs. How would the passage change if the writer were telling us not just about Sandy but about Sandy and her sister? Begin with "Sandy and her sister, meanwhile, pursue," and write a new version. (See Answer Key, p. 106.)

C. Agreement in number occurs not only with simple present verbs but also with the following auxiliaries: *am/is/are; was/were; does/do; has/have.* Look at these examples, also from "Mr. Doherty Builds His Dream Life."

The river *was* thawing.
The buildings *were* in good shape.
My wife Sandy and I *have* finally found contentment here in the country.
I'*m* not making anywhere near as much money as I did when I *was* employed full time, but now we *don't* need as much either.

D. The verb agrees with the head noun of the subject even when the sentence contains additional information between the head noun and the verb.

The crime reported on the front page of all the newspapers last week *was* never solved.
The crimes reported on the front page of all the newspapers last week *were* never solved.

E. The following pronouns and quantifiers regularly require a *singular* verb: *everyone, everybody, someone, somebody, anyone, anybody, no one, nobody, something, each,* and *every.*

Examples:

Everybody *has* left.   Every student *wants* good grades.
Everyone *wants* to be liked.   Each of the children *wants* ice cream.
Somebody who *is* standing over there *wants* to speak next.

Look for examples of these words when you read, and note the verb form used.

F. When a sentence starts with *There* plus a form of *be,* the verb agrees with the head noun of the noun phrase that follows the verb. For example:

There *is* one *bottle* on the table.
There *are* two *bottles* on the table.
There *is* some *juice* on the table.
There *is* a *vase* of flowers on the table.

Note how the head noun determines agreement in sentences with *a lot of:*

There *are* a lot of *people* in the room.
There *is* a lot of *money* in my bag.

Decide whether to use *is* or *are* in the following sentences:

1. There _____ some apples in the bowl on the table.
2. There _____ some money in my wallet.

3. There _____ a carton of milk in the refrigerator.
4. There _____ a box of books in the basement.
5. There _____ a lot of voters in rural regions.
6. There _____ a lot of food on the shelves.
7. There _____ a few coffee cups in the dishwasher.
8. There _____ no knives in the drawer.
9. There _____ no furniture in the room.
10. There _____ many serious problems that the voters in this
    district have to face.

(See Answer Key, p. 106.)

G. When a sentence has a *compound subject* (i.e., more than one subject), the verb must be plural in form:

My sister *visits* me every year. (subject: sister)
My aunt and my sister *visit* me every year. (compound subject: aunt and
    sister)

H. When you write a relative clause beginning with *who, which,* or *that,* look for its *referent*—the word that *who, which,* or *that* refers back to. The referent determines whether the verb should be singular or plural. For example:

The *people* in my class *who are* studying English *do* a lot of extra reading.

The *student* in my class *who is* sitting in the corner usually *does* a lot of
    extra reading.

See also Troublespot 16, "Relative Clauses."

I. For pronoun agreement (when to use *this/these, his/her,* and so on), see Troublespot 11, "Pronouns."

Editing Advice

If you have a problem with agreement of subject and verb, look at each troublesome verb you have written and ask the following questions:

> **Is the verb a present-tense form (-s form or "no -s" form), or does the verb phrase begin with one of the following auxiliaries: *does/do, has/have, am/are/ is,* or *was/were?***

(Flowchart continued)

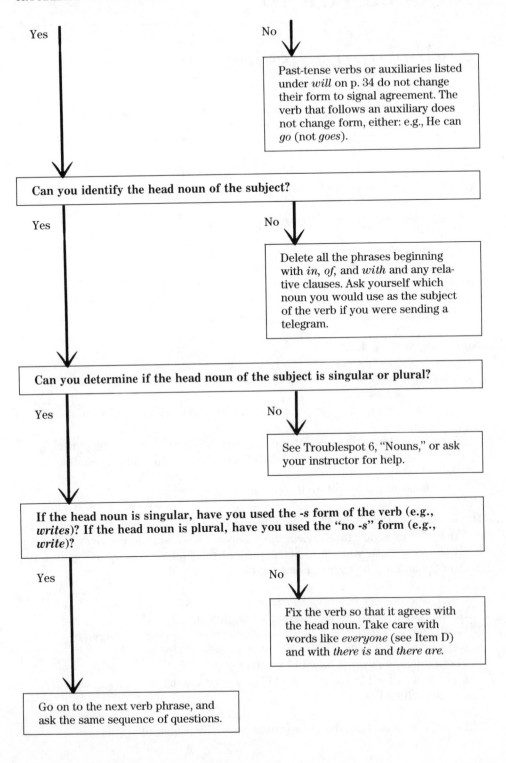

Yes   No

Past-tense verbs or auxiliaries listed under *will* on p. 34 do not change their form to signal agreement. The verb that follows an auxiliary does not change form, either: e.g., He can *go* (not *goes*).

Can you identify the head noun of the subject?

Yes   No

Delete all the phrases beginning with *in, of,* and *with* and any relative clauses. Ask yourself which noun you would use as the subject of the verb if you were sending a telegram.

Can you determine if the head noun of the subject is singular or plural?

Yes   No

See Troublespot 6, "Nouns," or ask your instructor for help.

If the head noun is singular, have you used the *-s* form of the verb (e.g., *writes*)? If the head noun is plural, have you used the "no *-s*" form (e.g., *write*)?

Yes   No

Fix the verb so that it agrees with the head noun. Take care with words like *everyone* (see Item D) and with *there is* and *there are.*

Go on to the next verb phrase, and ask the same sequence of questions.

Active and Passive

> *Question:* **How do I decide when to use a verb in the passive voice, and what must I remember about how to use it?**

A. The following sentence has a verb in the active voice:

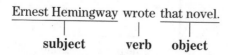

Ernest Hemingway wrote that novel.
     subject   **verb**   **object**

We can change the emphasis by rewriting the sentence like this:

That novel was written by Ernest Hemingway.

Note what we have done:

> We have made the original subject, *Ernest Hemingway,* less important in the sentence.
> We have reversed the order of the subject and object of the original sentence.
> We have changed the verb form to a form of *be* followed by the participle (see also Troublespot 8, "Verb Forms," and Appendix, "Irregular Verbs.")
> We have added *by* before the original subject.

B. Sometimes writers overuse the passive voice, which makes their writing flat and dull. But there are times when the passive is necessary to convey your meaning. Use the passive when it is not important to emphasize or even mention the doer of the action (the *agent*). For example:

> Good! The garbage *has been collected.*
> He *was promoted* to vice-president a month ago.
> When gold *was discovered* in the area, new towns sprang up overnight.
> Her performance *is being watched* very closely.
> These tomatoes *were grown* in New Jersey.
> I *was told* to send the form to you. [The writer doesn't want to say who did the telling.]

If the agent is important, the active voice is usually preferable:

Two old prospectors discovered gold in the area.

Not

Gold was discovered in the area by two old prospectors.

C. The passive occurs frequently in the following instances:

1. In scientific writing:

   The experiment was performed in 1983.

2. In journalism, or other writing, when the writer cannot or does not want to identify the agent:

   Jewelry worth five hundred thousand dollars was stolen from the Hotel Eldorado late last night.

3. When the action is more important than who did it. For example, in "The Paper Workingstuff" Russell Baker writes the following sentences:

   In the common everyday job, nothing is made any more.
   Very little is repaired.
   The buyer is encouraged to throw the thing away.

   In these sentences, *who* makes, repairs, or encourages is not what is important.

4. In a sentence in which the subject refers back to something mentioned in the previous sentence:

   In the common everyday job, nothing is made any more. Things are now made by machines. (Russell Baker)

   Things forms a link with *nothing* in the previous sentence, and thus gives the two sentences more cohesion than if a new subject had been introduced, as in the sentence:

   Machines now make things.

D. The form and sequence of passive verbs is often a problem for students writing in a second language. Look at the examples in the following list.

Active	*Passive*
They paint the house every three years.	The house *is painted* every three years.
They painted the house last year.	The house *was painted* last year.

Active	*Passive*
They will paint the house next year.	The house *will be painted* next year.
They are painting the house now.	The house *is being painted* now.
They were painting the house all last week.	The house *was being painted* all last week.
They have just painted the house.	The house *has just been painted.*
They had just painted the house when the roof collapsed.	The house *had just been painted* when the roof collapsed.
They will have painted the house by next Tuesday.	The house *will have been painted* by next Tuesday.

Note that in all the passive sentences, we use a form of *be* plus a participle. In addition, a *be* form can be joined by other auxiliaries.

The house *should be painted.*
The house *might have been painted* last year: I'm not sure if it was.

E. Read the following three selections from magazine articles. Write down all the verbs and indicate which verbs are active and which are passive.

1. Consider the typical twelve-story glass building in the typical American city. Nothing is being made in this building and nothing is being repaired, including the building itself. Constructed as a piece of junk, the building will be discarded when it wears out, and another piece of junk will be set in its place. (Russell Baker, "The Paper Workingstuff")
2. None of us will ever forget that first winter. We were buried under five feet of snow from December through March. (Jim Doherty, "Mr. Doherty Builds His Dream Life")
3. One thing is certain about tomorrow's job markets: dramatic shifts will occur in employment patterns. These changes are going to affect how we work and how we are educated and trained for jobs . . . . The essence of Japan's problem is that . . . 20 percent of the entire work force will retire at 80 percent of their base pay for the rest of their lives. Japan was forced to go robotic to remain competitive. The United States, too, will be filling many of today's blue-collar jobs with robots. (Marvin J. Cetron, "Getting Ready for the Jobs of the Future")

(See Answer Key, p. 106.)

F. Write a paragraph describing what you were taught about the English language and about writing in your previous schools. After you have written your paragraph, look carefully at the verbs you used. Did you use the passive or the active? Why did you make the choices you made?

Editing Advice

When you want to examine closely whether you have correctly used a verb in the passive voice, ask these questions:

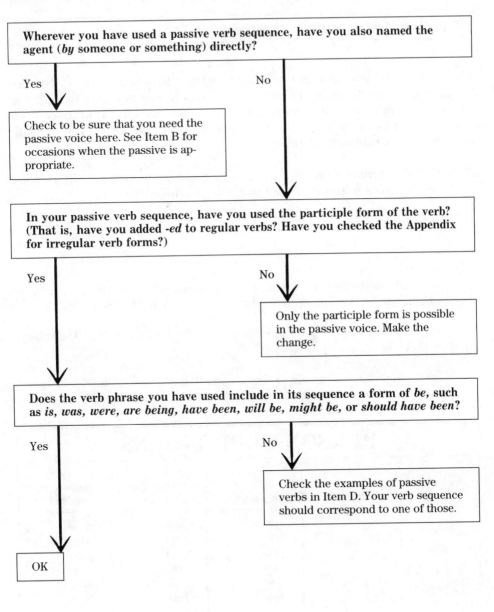

Wherever you have used a passive verb sequence, have you also named the agent (*by* someone or something) directly?

Yes   No

Check to be sure that you need the passive voice here. See Item B for occasions when the passive is appropriate.

In your passive verb sequence, have you used the participle form of the verb? (That is, have you added *-ed* to regular verbs? Have you checked the Appendix for irregular verb forms?)

Yes   No

Only the participle form is possible in the passive voice. Make the change.

Does the verb phrase you have used include in its sequence a form of *be*, such as *is, was, were, are being, have been, will be, might be,* or *should have been*?

Yes   No

Check the examples of passive verbs in Item D. Your verb sequence should correspond to one of those.

OK

TROUBLESPOT 11

Pronouns

> **Question:** How do I know which pronoun to use?

A. The forms of pronouns are rule-governed; that is, which forms to use are determined by specific rules. The box below shows the rule-governed forms of the personal pronouns. No other forms are possible. Note carefully the form *its*. Even though it indicates possession, there is no apostrophe. Do not confuse *its* with *it's*, which is the contracted form of *it is*.

B. In English, a pronoun agrees in gender (male, female, or neuter) with the noun it refers back to (its *referent*) and not with the noun following it:

My father never visits *his* aunt.

My mother often visits *her* uncle.

C. Other troublesome forms are demonstrative pronouns or adjectives. These are used to point out (or "demonstrate") what you are referring to. (See p. 47.)

Look at the following four passages from articles and books. Answer the question that follows each passage.

1. One would expect people to cherish paintings because of their beauty and originality, or because of the artist's skills; in short, for aesthetic rea-

PERSONAL PRONOUNS

Subject pronoun	*Object pronoun*	*Possessive adjective (+ noun)*	*Possessive pronoun*	*Reflexive pronoun*
I	me	my	mine	myself
we	us	our	ours	ourselves
you	you	your	yours	yourself
you	you	your	yours	yourselves
he	him	his	his	himself
she	her	her	hers	herself
it	it	its	–	itself
they	them	their	theirs	themselves
one	one/him/her	one's	–	oneself

Demonstrative Adjectives or Pronouns	
Singular	*Plural*
this	these
that	those

sons. Yet only 16 percent of the time were any of *those* characteristics mentioned. (Csikszentmihalyi and Rochberg-Halton, "Object Lessons")

Which characteristics does the author mean?

2. If someone wore shoes with run-over heels, or shoes that had not been shined for a long time, or shoes with broken laces, you could be pretty sure *this* person would be slovenly in other things as well. (Evan S. Connell, *Mrs. Bridge*)

Which person is the writer referring to?

3. Most of all, though, I worried about facing my mother. Even as I write *that* sentence, I feel it sounds unfair. (Susan Allen Toth, *Ivy Days*)

Which sentence is the author referring to?

4. Right now, women still hold only 6 percent of middle-management positions and one percent of jobs in upper management. But *this* will change, says one female executive . . . . (Mary Schnack, "Are Women Bosses Better?")

What does *this* refer to?

(See Answer Key, p. 106.)

D. In the following selection from an article, "Treasures" by Joan Costello, circle any personal pronouns or demonstratives that you find. Then decide what word in the passage each pronoun refers to. Draw a line from the circled pronoun to its referent—that is, the word (or words) to which it refers. Note the use of *it is* to begin a sentence and to direct the reader's attention to what comes next. Do not circle that use of *it*. Finally, note that the word *that* can also be used to introduce clauses (see Troublespot 3, "Combining Sentences: Subordinating").

Children form attachments to objects at an early age. Most children select a

blanket or toy animal to cherish. Usually it is one that they have nearby as

they fall asleep. Typically the object evokes a sense of comfort and its soothing qualities may substitute somewhat for the attention of loved ones.

As children grow, their early attachments to blankets or teddy bears fade

and they invest other objects with special meanings. It is often unclear why

they choose certain objects over others; nor is it clear even to them pre-

cisely what these things mean.

(See Answer Key, p. 107.)

Editing Advice

Look at each problematic pronoun in your essay, and ask these questions:

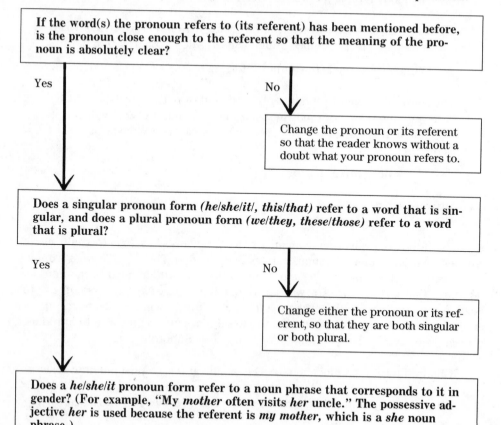

If the word(s) the pronoun refers to (its referent) has been mentioned before, is the pronoun close enough to the referent so that the meaning of the pronoun is absolutely clear?

Yes   No

Change the pronoun or its referent so that the reader knows without a doubt what your pronoun refers to.

Does a singular pronoun form *(he/she/it, this/that)* refer to a word that is singular, and does a plural pronoun form *(we/they, these/those)* refer to a word that is plural?

Yes   No

Change either the pronoun or its referent, so that they are both singular or both plural.

Does a *he/she/it* pronoun form refer to a noun phrase that corresponds to it in gender? (For example, "My *mother* often visits *her* uncle." The possessive adjective *her* is used because the referent is *my mother,* which is a *she* noun phrase.)

(Flowchart continued)

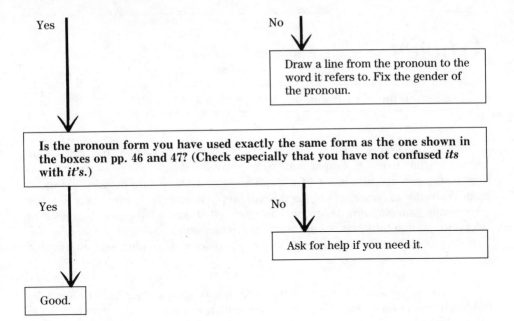

Yes

No

Draw a line from the pronoun to the word it refers to. Fix the gender of the pronoun.

Is the pronoun form you have used exactly the same form as the one shown in the boxes on pp. 46 and 47? (Check especially that you have not confused *its* with *it's*.)

Yes

No

Ask for help if you need it.

Good.

TROUBLESPOT 12

Articles

> *Question:* **When do I use *a, an, the,* or no article at all?**

Other languages do not use articles the way that English does, so some second-language writers find articles to be troublesome. While there are rules to help you, there are also a lot of exceptions and a lot of fine distinctions to be made. You should not expect to learn a rule, apply it, and then never make another error again. Learning how to use articles correctly takes a long time. You need to read a lot, notice how articles are used, and make notes about what you observe. You should also study and refer to the explanations, examples, and charts that follow.

A. The article you use depends on the noun it modifies, so you have to begin by looking at the noun and making the following distinctions (see also Troublespot 6, "Nouns"):

1. Is it a *common* or *proper* noun? A proper noun is the name of a specific person, place, or thing (e.g., *James Raimes; Hunter College; England*). All proper nouns begin with a capital letter. Other nouns are common nouns (e.g., *man, school, country*). For the most part, singular proper nouns are not preceded by an article (however, see Item D in this chapter). Plural proper nouns are preceded by *the,* as in *the Great Lakes* and *the United States.*

2. If the noun is a common noun, is it *countable* or *uncountable* in the sentence in which you want to use it? Examples of countable nouns are:

chair (a chair, two chairs)
meal (one meal, three meals)
machine (a machine, some machines)

Uncountable, or mass and abstract nouns, include, for example:

furniture	information	honesty
rice	gravity	fun
machinery	pollution	vocabulary
equipment	satisfaction	traffic
advice	knowledge	homework

(See also Items C and D in Troublespot 6, "Nouns.")

Difficulty with articles occurs with common nouns because what is considered countable and uncountable varies from language to language. In Spanish, for example, the equivalent of *furniture* is a countable word; in English, *furniture* is always uncountable. It has no plural form, and we cannot say *a furniture*.

Most grammar books list nouns that are regularly uncountable in English. However, someone else's list is never as useful to you as your own. As you continue to read and write in English, keep a list of any uncountable nouns you come across.

B. Next, decide whether a common noun, in your sentence context, has a specific or a nonspecific reference for the writer and the reader.

1. A *specific* reference is known by the writer and by the reader as something unique, specific, or familiar, or previously identified to the reader.

   Example A: My daughter is looking after *the dog* this week.

   The writer here expects the reader to know precisely which dog is meant: the family's dog, or a dog the writer has previously identified and perhaps described.

   Example B: My neighbor bought *a dog*. My daughter is looking after *the dog* this week.

   Here the dog is identified as the specific dog that the neighbor bought.

   Example C: *The dogs* in the backyard are very dangerous.

   The reader knows specifically which dogs: the ones that are in the backyard.

2. A *nonspecific* reference is not identified by the writer and by the reader as something known, unique, or familiar.

   Example A: My daughter is looking after *a dog* this week.

   Here the writer does not expect the reader to know about the dog in question. It could be any dog—a neighbor's dog, a schoolmate's dog, a poodle, a spaniel, or a sheepdog.

   Example B: *Dogs* are friendly animals.

   Here the writer is making a generalization about all dogs everywhere.

   Example C: *Some dogs* can be trained to be attack dogs.

   Here the writer is not making a generalization about all dogs, but limiting the statement with a quantity word.

C. Once you have made these distinctions about the noun in the context of the meaning of your sentence, you can then apply some general rules about article use. But beware! Article use is complex. The accompanying box offers only general guidelines to help you decide which articles to use with common nouns. There are many cases that you just have to learn one by one. So, whenever you find an exception to a rule, write it down.

Note: The important things to remember as you work with the box are:

1. A countable singular noun *must have an article (a/an or the)* or some other determiner (e.g., *this, her, every*) in front of it. A countable singular noun *never stands alone;* that is, in a sentence, *book* by itself is not possible. So, you must write:

   > a book
   > the book
   > this/that book
   > my/his/etc., book
   > every/each book

2. Uncountable nouns are *never* used with *a/an.* Therefore, forms such as **a furniture, *an advice,* or **an information* are not possible. To express the concept of amounts of these uncountable nouns, we have to use expressions such as *two pieces of furniture, several types of food, three teaspoons of sugar, some items of information,* or *a piece of equipment.* (See also Troublespot 6, "Nouns.")

3. Some nouns can be determined as countable or uncountable only in the context of the sentence in which they are used. For example:

ARTICLES WITH COMMON NOUNS

Type of noun	Reference for writer and reader	
	Specific	*Nonspecific*
Countable singular	the	a/an
Countable plural	the	Quantity words (*some, a few, many,* etc.). See p. 25 in Troublespot 6, "Nouns." *or* No article with a generalization.
Uncountable	the	Quantity words (*some, a little,* etc.). See p. 25 in Troublespot 6, "Nouns." *or* No article with a generalization.

Life can be hard when you are old. (Here *life* is generic and un-countable; the writer is making a generalization.)

My grandmother lived *a happy life.* (Here *life* is countable; the writer sees different types of lives: *a happy life, an unhappy life, a useful life,* etc.)

So, what you intend as you write determines the category of countable/uncountable. Only occasionally is it fixed within the word itself.

D. Note some word groups that cause difficulties:

Unique objects: *the earth, the sun, the moon,* but *Earth*
Places: *France, Central Park, San Francisco, Mount Vesuvius, McDonald's,*
     but *the United States of America, the United Kingdom, the Sahara
     (Desert), The Hague, the Statue of Liberty*
Oceans, rivers, seas, and lakes: *the Pacific, the Amazon, the Mediterranean,
     the Great Lakes,* but *Lake Superior*
Diseases and ailments: *a cold, a headache, the flu,* but *pneumonia, cancer*
Destination: *to go to the store, to go to the post office, to go to the bank, to go
     to school, to go to church, to go to bed, to go home*
Locations: *at home, in bed, in school, in college*
Expressions of time: *in the morning, in the evening* (but *at night), all the
     time, most of the time* (but *sometimes, in time, on time)*

When trying to decide whether to use an article, ask for help if you need it. Every time you learn a new use of an article, write it down.

E. Examine the passage that appears in Troublespot 7, Item C, p. 31. Underline each noun, along with any articles or other determiners used (see Item B in Troublespot 6 for a list of determiners). Try to fit each article or determiner + noun into one of the categories in the box on p. 52. Write down the categories to which you would assign the determiners and nouns:

Countable or uncountable?
If countable, singular or plural?
Specific or nonspecific reference? (Note that demonstratives and posses-
     sives give a specific reference.)

(See Answer Key, p. 107.)

F. Read a newspaper or magazine article every few days. Underline all the nouns and articles and try to explain why the writer chose to use the article form that appears. This frequent close examination will help you understand the relationships between articles and the concepts they express.

Editing Advice

If you have problems deciding on *a/an/the* or no article at all, look at each troublesome noun phrase and ask the following questions:

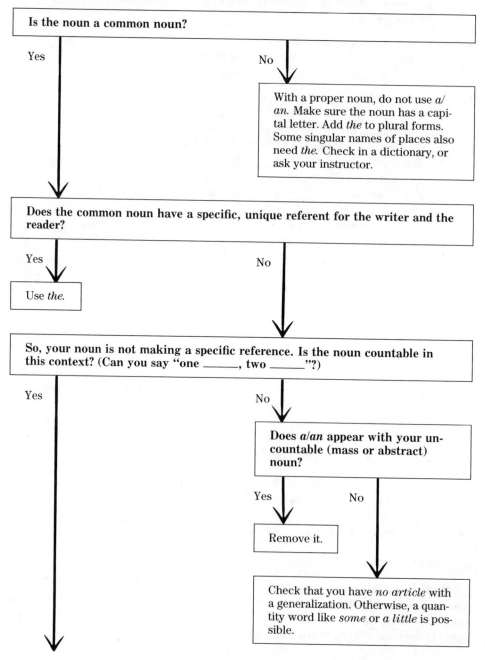

> **Is the noun a common noun?**

Yes　　　　　　　　　　　　　　No

> With a proper noun, do not use *a/ an*. Make sure the noun has a capital letter. Add *the* to plural forms. Some singular names of places also need *the*. Check in a dictionary, or ask your instructor.

> **Does the common noun have a specific, unique referent for the writer and the reader?**

Yes　　　　　　　　　　　　　　No

> Use *the*.

> **So, your noun is not making a specific reference. Is the noun countable in this context? (Can you say "one _____, two _____"?)**

Yes　　　　　　　　　　　　　　No

> **Does *a/an* appear with your un-countable (mass or abstract) noun?**

Yes　　　　　　　　No

> Remove it.

> Check that you have *no article* with a generalization. Otherwise, a quantity word like *some* or *a little* is possible.

(Flowchart continued)

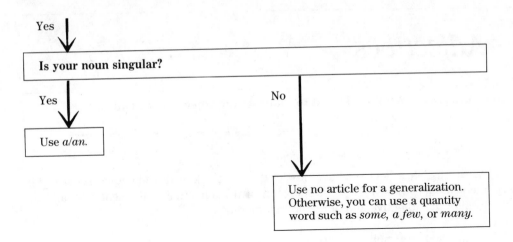

Yes

Is your noun singular?

Yes

Use *a/an*.

No

Use no article for a generalization.
Otherwise, you can use a quantity
word such as *some, a few,* or *many.*

TROUBLESPOT 13

Adjectives

> *Question:* **What do I need to know about adjectives to edit my writing?**

A. In English, adjectives have no plural form. Look at the adjective *important* in the sentences below. Note the position of the adjective in the sentence, and the form of the adjective and of the noun it modifies.

> An *important* politician attended the conference.
> Some *important* politicians attended the conference.
> The politicians who attended the conference are *important.*

B. We add endings to short adjectives when we form comparatives or superlatives:

> Sally is smart and witty. She is smart*er* and witt*ier* than her sister.
> She was the smart*est* in her class, but not the witt*iest.*

C. But when the adjective is long (i.e., three syllables), we use *more* for the comparative and *the most* for the superlative:

> She was *more serious* about her work than other students, and she was *the most ambitious* student in her class.

D. Adjectives expressing nationality always have a capital letter:

> a *French* film
> a *Chinese* restaurant

E. Adjectives in a series tend to occur in a certain order, as indicated in the box on p. 57. However, there can be frequent exceptions.

F. Look carefully at each of the following noun phrases, and determine which category in the following box each word belongs to:

> 1. that sophisticated young Italian model
> 2. his comfortable white velvet couch
> 3. two middle-aged Catholic bishops
> 4. their charming little wood cabin

Determiner	Opinion	Physical description				Nationality	Religion	Material	Noun	Head noun
		Size	Shape	Age	Color					
three	beautiful			old						houses
my			long		blue			silk	evening	gown
a	delicious					French				meal
her		big		old		English		oak	writing	desk
Lee's	charming						Catholic			teacher
several		little	round					marble	coffee	tables

(See Answer Key, p. 108.)

G. Examine the following *adjective + noun* sequences, and determine the category of each adjective according to the box above.

1. table top
2. plastic beads
3. a little silver elephant
4. a French meal
5. a little tin replica
6. a circular straw place mat
7. three buffalo hides
8. an ancient ivory bracelet

(See Answer Key, p. 108.)

H. Some adjectives used after a verb phrase *(predicate adjectives)* are regularly used with prepositions:

I am *afraid of* ghosts.
I confess that I am *proud of* winning the race.

Whenever you come across a *predicate adjective + preposition* in your reading, write down the whole sentence in which it appears. Here are some to start off your list:

aware of   interested in
suspicious of   different from

fond of   full of

satisfied with   jealous of

happy about

Editing Advice

If you are unsure about your use of an adjective at any point in your writing, ask these questions:

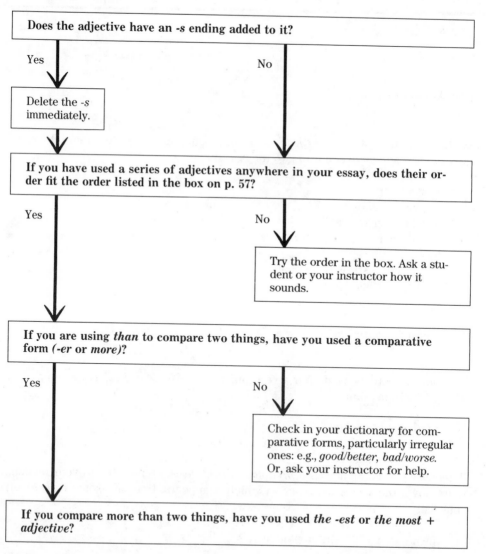

Does the adjective have an *-s* ending added to it?

Yes   No

Delete the *-s* immediately.

If you have used a series of adjectives anywhere in your essay, does their order fit the order listed in the box on p. 57?

Yes   No

Try the order in the box. Ask a student or your instructor how it sounds.

If you are using *than* to compare two things, have you used a comparative form *(-er* or *more)*?

Yes   No

Check in your dictionary for comparative forms, particularly irregular ones: e.g., *good/better, bad/worse.* Or, ask your instructor for help.

If you compare more than two things, have you used *the -est* or *the most +* adjective?

(Flowchart continued)

Yes

No

Check in your dictionary for the form of the superlative, especially irregular forms like *the best* and *the worst*. Ask for help if you need it.

Good.

Adverbs

Question: **How can I tell whether to use an adjective or an adverb, and how do I use an adverb in a sentence?**

A. Adjectives tell us about nouns:

The *comfortable* chair is in the corner.

The chair in the corner $\begin{cases} \text{looks} \\ \text{seems} \\ \text{is} \end{cases}$ *comfortable.*

Comfortable tells us *what kind of* chair it is.

Adverbs tell us about verbs:

He was sitting *comfortably.*

Comfortably tells us *how* he was sitting.

Adverbs also tell us about adjectives:

She was *conspicuously* silent.

The adverb tells us *in what way* she was silent.

They were *noticeably* angry.

The adverb tells us *in what way* they were angry.

B. A common adverb ending is *-ly.* Occasionally, however, *-ly* will be found on words that are *not* adverbs, such as *friendly* and *lovely,* so be careful.

C. Write down the adverb forms of the following adjectives: *happy, simple, careful, successful, fortunate, basic, angry, possible.* If necessary, use your dictionary to help you.

(See Answer Key, p. 109.)

D. Adverbs that tell us how an action occurs can appear in different positions in a sentence. Note the following:

Adverb	*Subject*	*Adverb*	*Verb + Object*	*Adverb*
Systematically,	the teacher		reviewed the tenses.	
	The teacher		reviewed the tenses	systematically.
	The teacher	systematically	reviewed the tenses.	

But while an adverb can be moved around in a sentence, it can *never* be placed between the verb and a short object. The following sentence is not acceptable in English:

*The teacher reviewed *systematically* the tenses.

E. Another type of adverb that can be moved around in a sentence is one that tells us about the whole sentence: for example, *fortunately, actually, obviously, certainly,* and *recently.*

Certainly, he is very intelligent.
He is *certainly* very intelligent.
He is very intelligent, *certainly.*

F. Many adverbs of frequency tell us about the whole sentence and not just about the verb. They do not always end in *-ly* and can be placed in different positions in the sentence. These adverbs include *always, sometimes, often, seldom, usually,* and *frequently.* For example:

She is *always* tactful. (after single *be* verb)
She *always* behaves tactfully. (before single verb)
She has *always* spoken tactfully to her boss. (after first auxiliary verb)

G. Choose a few paragraphs from an article in a newspaper or magazine. Circle any adjectives you find and underline any adverbs. Then, on a piece of paper, make two columns and write down both the adjective and the adverb forms of all the words you find.

Editing Advice

If you are worried about whether you have used an adverb correctly, ask yourself the following questions:

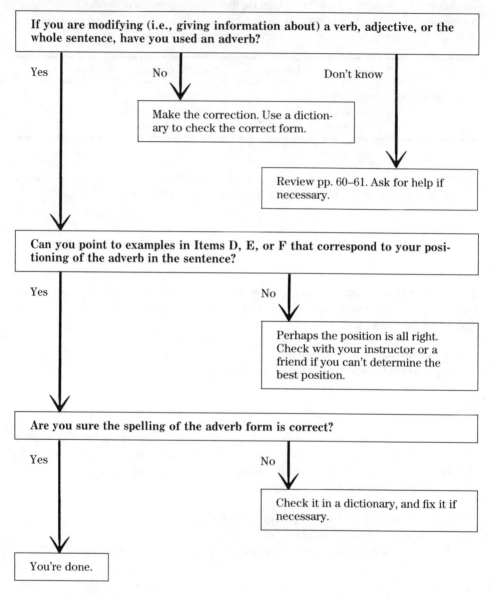

If you are modifying (i.e., giving information about) a verb, adjective, or the whole sentence, have you used an adverb?

Yes   No   Don't know

Make the correction. Use a dictionary to check the correct form.

Review pp. 60–61. Ask for help if necessary.

Can you point to examples in Items D, E, or F that correspond to your positioning of the adverb in the sentence?

Yes   No

Perhaps the position is all right. Check with your instructor or a friend if you can't determine the best position.

Are you sure the spelling of the adverb form is correct?

Yes   No

Check it in a dictionary, and fix it if necessary.

You're done.

-ing *and Participle Forms*

> **Question:** How can I avoid errors with *-ing* forms and participle *(-ed/-en)* forms?

A. Word forms that end with *-ing* are used in the following ways:

1. As part of a complete active verb phrase, with one or more auxiliaries:

   He is
   He was
   He will be   paint*ing* the house.
   He should be
   He has been
   etc.

   (See also pp. 29–30 in Troublespot 7, "Verb Tenses.")

2. To include additional information in the sentence:

   The woman *wearing* blue jeans is his sister.
   (The woman is wearing blue jeans.)

   Walking as quickly as I could, I managed to get out of sight.
   (I was walking quickly.)

   Hurrying along the street, I saw them get into their car.
   (I was hurrying.)

   I saw him *hurrying* along the street.
   (He was hurrying.)

   She left early, *promising* to return soon.
   (She promised to return.)

   Driving over the bridge, we admired the lights of the city.
   (We were driving.)

   But not *Driving over the bridge, the lights looked beautiful.
   (Why not? Because the lights weren't driving!)

   Note how all these *-ing* phrases express an active meaning.

3. As adjectives (with active meaning):

a *crying* baby (The baby is crying.)
an *interesting* movie (The movie interested us.)
The play was very *boring*. (The play bored us.)
The race was *exhausting*. (The race exhausted the runners.)

4. As nouns (*-ing* nouns are called *gerunds*):

a. As the subject of the sentence:

Swimming is good for you.
Driving on icy roads is dangerous.

b. As the object of certain verbs:

She *dislikes swimming.*
He *enjoys playing* tennis.
She *avoids driving* on icy roads.
He *finished cooking* dinner at 8 P.M.
The thief *denied having* taken the television.
They *postponed holding* the meeting.

There are other verbs regularly followed by the *-ing* noun form. Note them as you come across them in your reading.

c. After prepositions:

They insisted *on paying* for themselves.
She is capable *of handling* the job.

Verb phrases with preposition + *-ing* include:

approve of	get (be) used to
blame for	look forward to
complain about	suspect of
get (be) accustomed to	thank for

5. In idiomatic expressions with the verb *go:*

to go shopping	to go skating/skiing/bowling
to go fishing	to go swimming
to go dancing	to go sightseeing

B. Participles (*-ed/-en* words) are used in the following ways:

1. As part of a complete active verb phrase with *have* auxiliaries:

He *has painted* the house.
They *had painted* the house before I arrived.

See also Troublespot 8, "Verb Forms."

2. As part of a complete passive verb phrase with *be/being* auxiliaries:

The house
{
is
is being
was
was being
will be
should be
has been
had been
might be
might have been
etc.
}
painted.

(See also Troublespot 10, "Active and Passive.")

3. To add information to a sentence:

Confused by the people and traffic, Jack wandered around for hours before he found his sister's apartment building.
(Jack was confused.)

Begun five years ago, the building had never progressed beyond the foundation.
(The building was begun five years ago.)

When *confronted* with financial problems, many people simply make more and more use of their credit cards.
(When people are confronted with financial problems, they . . .)

The food *prepared* in that restaurant is very exotic.
(The food that is prepared by the chef in that restaurant is very exotic.)

Note that all the preceding participial phrases express a passive meaning.

4. As adjectives (with passive meaning):

an *exhausted* swimmer
The swimmer was *exhausted* after the race.
The *exhausted* swimmer collapsed after the race.

C. Sometimes writers mix up the *-ing* and *-ed/-en* forms. Study these correct sentences:

Football *interests* a lot of people. (*Interests* is a verb.)

Football is an *interesting* sport.
Football is *interesting* to Pat's two children.
Pat's children are *interested* in football.
Interested in the match, the children stayed home from school to watch it.

D. Write as many sentences as you can using each of the following groups of words. Use the past-tense verb form, the *-ing* form, and the participle *(-ed/-en)* forms of the first word of each group. Add any other words you need.

1. annoy	Julie	the loud radio
2. confuse	the students	the difficult lecture
3. surprise	we (or) us	the end of the movie

(See Answer Key, p. 109.)

E. In the following passages from magizine articles, fill in the *-ing* or the participle form of the given verb. Use the Appendix to check irregular participle forms.

1. Just as many of us are aware of *(save)* _____ special things to pre-serve memories or enhance relationships, we've also felt that by *(get rid)* _____ of gifts, photos, letters, we're *(mark)* _____ the end of a period or relationship. (Barbara Lang Stern, "Lure of Possessions")

2. When I watch Emily *(collect)* _____ eggs in the evening, *(fish)* _____ with Jim on the river or *(enjoy)* _____ an old-fash-ioned picnic in the orchard with the entire family, I know we've *(find)* _____ just what we were *(look)* _____ for. (Jim Doherty, "Mr. Doherty Builds His Dream Life")

3. *(Construct)* _____ as a piece of junk, the building will be *(discard)* _____ when it wears out, and another piece of junk will be *(set)* _____ in its place. (Russell Baker, "The Paper Workingstuff")

4. Japan was *(force)* _____ to go robotic to remain competitive. The

United States, too, will be *(fill)* _____ many of today's blue-collar jobs

with robots. The *(displace)* _____ workers will have to learn the new

skills necessary to build and maintain the robots. (Marvin J. Cetron, "Getting Ready

for the Jobs of the Future")

5. What is clear is that few such men exist today, although women still seem

(surprise) _____ and *(disappoint)* _____ when they can't

find them. (William Novak, "What Do Women Really Want?")

(See Answer Key, p. 109.)

F. Rewrite the following pairs of sentences as one sentence by using an *-ing* or a participle phrase to include the first sentence in the second. Make the second sentence your new independent clause. For example:

He felt hungry.
He bought three slices of pizza.
New sentence: Feeling very hungry, he bought three slices of pizza.

1. She wanted to get the job.
   She arrived early for the interview.

2. The gray-haired man is wearing a blue coat.
   The gray-haired man is my father. (Begin with "The gray-haired man.")

3. The movie excited us.
   We saw a movie last week.

4. The student was confused by the examination questions.
   The student failed the exam.

5. A painting was stolen from the museum yesterday.
   The painting was extremely valuable.

6. The little boy was asked to share his toys.
   The little boy screamed and cried.

7. She played in the tennis tournament.
   She twisted her ankle.

(See Answer Key, p. 109.)

Editing Advice

If you have problems with *-ing* and participle forms, ask the following questions about each troublesome sentence:

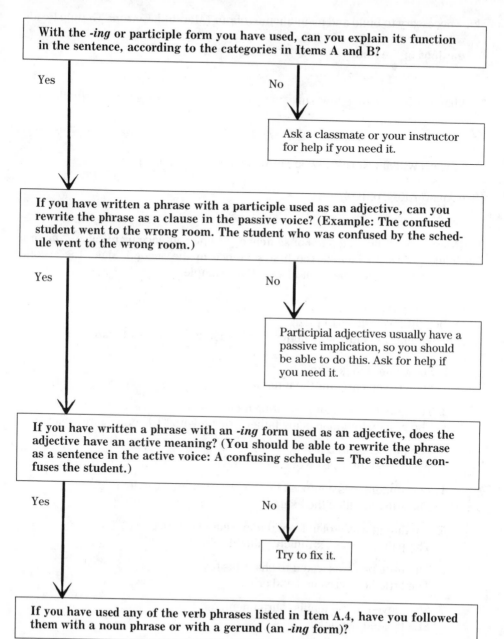

With the *-ing* or participle form you have used, can you explain its function in the sentence, according to the categories in Items A and B?

Yes No

Ask a classmate or your instructor for help if you need it.

If you have written a phrase with a participle used as an adjective, can you rewrite the phrase as a clause in the passive voice? (Example: The confused student went to the wrong room. The student who was confused by the schedule went to the wrong room.)

Yes No

Participial adjectives usually have a passive implication, so you should be able to do this. Ask for help if you need it.

If you have written a phrase with an *-ing* form used as an adjective, does the adjective have an active meaning? (You should be able to rewrite the phrase as a sentence in the active voice: A confusing schedule = The schedule confuses the student.)

Yes No

Try to fix it.

If you have used any of the verb phrases listed in Item A.4, have you followed them with a noun phrase or with a gerund (an *-ing* form)?

(Flowchart continued)

Yes

No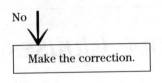

Make the correction.

Well done.

TROUBLESPOT 16

Relative Clauses

> *Question:* **What do I need to know about clauses with *who, whom, whose, which,* and *that*?**

A. Relative clauses tell the reader more about a noun phrase:

The boy kept looking at his watch.
(The boy was waiting at the corner.)
The boy *who was waiting at the corner* kept looking at his watch.

The independent clause is *The boy kept looking at his watch.* The clause *who was waiting on the corner* tells the reader more about *the boy;* it tells the reader which boy we mean.

B. A relative clause is combined with (or *embedded in*) an independent clause in the following way, with the relative clause following its referent (the head noun it refers back to):

1. I bought the suit.
   (The suit made me look thinner.)
   I bought the suit *that made me look thinner.*
2. I bought the suit.
   (My mother liked the suit.)
   I bought the suit *that my mother liked.*
   or I bought the suit *my mother liked.*
   That can be omitted if the pronoun is the object of its own clause. See Item D.
3. The person was wearing a blue suit. [I took over the person's job.]
   The person *whose job I took over* was wearing a blue suit.

C. The relative pronouns *who, which,* and *that* can refer back to singular or plural noun phrases. When *who, which,* or *that* is the subject of its relative clause, the verb of that clause agrees with the noun phrase that the pronoun refers back to:

The *journalist who wants* to interview you *works* for a newsmagazine.

The *journalists who want* to interview you *work* for a newsmagazine.

Note that we do *not* repeat the subject of the sentence—*journalist(s)*—after the relative clause. The following sentence is *wrong* in English:

*The journalists who want to interview you *they* work for a newsmagazine.

They should be omitted here. The subject of the verb *work*—that is, *journalists*—has already been stated.

D. When the relative pronoun—*who(m), which, that*—is the object of its own clause, it can be omitted:

I bought the suit that my mother liked. (My mother liked the suit.)
I bought the suit my mother liked.
I didn't buy the suit (that) I really liked!

E. Sentences that combine prepositions with relative pronouns require special attention.

The woman is a teacher.
(My friend is talking to the woman.)

There are five possible ways to combine these sentences:

1. The woman *whom* my friend is talking *to* is a teacher.
2. The woman *who* my friend is talking *to* is a teacher.
(Some people now accept the *who* form in the object position in the relative clause. Others, however, insist on the first version (with *whom*), which is more formally "correct." Ask your instructor which form you should use in your writing.
3. The woman *that* my friend is talking *to* is a teacher.
4. The woman my friend is talking *to* is a teacher.
5. The woman *to whom* my friend is talking is a teacher.

Note that you cannot use *that* as a relative pronoun immediately after a preposition. In the last example, *whom* is the only pronoun possible after *to*.

F. Use the box on p. 72 to help you determine which relative pronoun to use. You see from the box that you can use the word *that* as a relative pronoun in both subject and object positions. There are times, however, when you *cannot* use *that* as the relative pronoun in these positions:

1. When the relative clause gives additional information about a unique person, thing, or event. The clause does not define or restrict which person, thing, or event the writer means, but adds information about a person or

Position within clause	Relative pronoun refers to:	
	people	*things/concepts*
subject	who that	which that
direct object	who/whom that (omitted)	which that (omitted)
possessive	whose	whose of which

thing that has already been identified. Relative clauses like this use *who,* *whom,* and *which;* they also have commas around them, as in these sentences:

Jessica's parents, who live nearby, are both lawyers.
Jessica is engaged to my brother, who is standing next to her in the photograph.
My brother always did better in school than Jessica, who never seemed to find time to do homework.
They met in Prospect Park, which is close to both their homes.

Note that in each case when commas are used, the referent is unique: *Jessica's parents, my brother, Jessica, Prospect Park.*
      If your referent is not a proper noun or a unique person or thing, then the relative clause is restrictive and you will not use commas (as in the examples in Items A through E). *When in doubt, leave the comma out.*

2. When the relative pronoun refers to the whole of the previous clause:

He moved to the country, which he had always wanted to do.

3. When the relative pronoun follows a preposition:

The controversy to which the author is referring has not yet been resolved.

G. Combine each of the following pairs of sentences into one sentence, using a relative clause. (Refer to the box in Item F if you need help.) Pay special attention to which of the two sentences you want to embed in the other. How does it change the sense of the sentence if you do it another way? Only one of these sentences will need commas around the relative clause. Which one is it?

1. The man was awarded a prize. The man won the race.
2. The girl is sitting in the front row. The girl asks a lot of questions.
3. The people are from California. I met the people at a party last night.
4. The house is gigantic. He is living in the house.
5. Ms. McHam lives next door to me. Ms. McHam is a lawyer.
6. The journalist has won a lot of prizes. You read the journalist's story yesterday.
7. The radio was made in Taiwan. I bought the radio.
8. She told her friends about the book. She had just read the book.
9. The man is a radio announcer. I am looking after the man's dog.

(See Answer Key, p. 109.)

H. Combine the following pairs of sentences by making the second sentence into a relative clause. Separate the clauses with a comma, because you are providing additional rather than necessary information. Introduce the relative clause with expressions like the following: *some of whom/which, one of whom/which, many of whom/which, none of whom/which, neither of whom/which, most of whom/which.* For example:

She has three sisters. None of them will help her.
She has three sisters, *none of whom* will help her.

1. At the lecture there were thirty-three people. Most of them lived in the neighborhood.
2. They waited half an hour for the committee members. Some of them just did not show up.
3. I sang three songs. One of them was "Singing in the Rain."
4. The statewide poetry competition was held last month, and she submitted four poems. None of them won a prize.
5. On every wall of his house, he has hundreds of books. Most of them are detective novels.

(See Answer Key, p. 110.)

Editing Advice

If you want to check that you have used a relative clause correctly, ask the following questions:

Can you identify both the independent clause and the relative clause in your sentence?

(Flowchart continued)

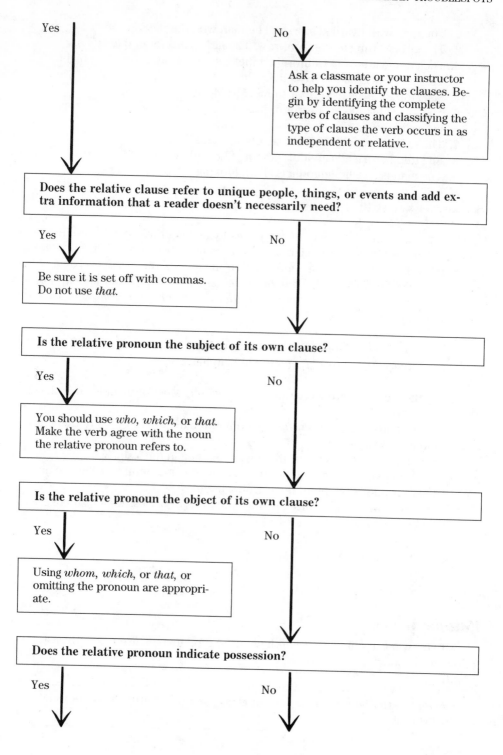

Yes

No

Ask a classmate or your instructor to help you identify the clauses. Begin by identifying the complete verbs of clauses and classifying the type of clause the verb occurs in as independent or relative.

Does the relative clause refer to unique people, things, or events and add extra information that a reader doesn't necessarily need?

Yes

No

Be sure it is set off with commas. Do not use *that*.

Is the relative pronoun the subject of its own clause?

Yes

No

You should use *who, which,* or *that*. Make the verb agree with the noun the relative pronoun refers to.

Is the relative pronoun the object of its own clause?

Yes

No

Using *whom, which,* or *that,* or omitting the pronoun are appropriate.

Does the relative pronoun indicate possession?

Yes

No

(Flowchart continued)

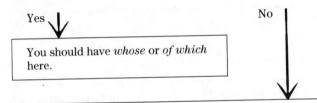

Yes

You should have *whose* or *of which* here.

No

Is the relative pronoun the object of a preposition?

Yes

Follow either of these patterns:

The apartment (that) she is living in is huge.
The apartment in which she is living is huge.

TROUBLESPOT 17

Conditions

> *Question:* **What do I need to be aware of when I write sentences with *if*?**

A. There are four types of conditions you can express:

fact
future prediction
speculation about present or future
past speculation (contrary to fact)

The type of condition you write depends upon the meaning you want to express.

1. The following sentences express conditions of *fact:*

   If cockroaches are not controlled, they multiply very quickly.
   If water freezes, it turns into ice.
   If you hear a quick "beep," it's the busy signal.
   If it's Thursday, I have to go to my exercise class.

2. The following sentences express conditions of *future prediction:*

   If the high divorce rate continues, many children will at some time in their lives be a part of a single-parent family.
   If I get promoted, I will be very happy.
   She might take the job if she can work a shorter day.

3. The following sentences express conditions of *present-future speculation:*

   If she gave up her job, her family finances would change dramatically for the worse.
   If I were Mayor, I'd do more to improve public transportation.
   If the mortgage rate were to go up next week, she wouldn't be able to finance her new apartment.
   If I had enough money, I would take a long vacation.
   If my grandparents were alive today, they would be shocked by that bathing suit.

When you write sentences like these, the reader should understand them in the following way:

If I had enough money—but I don't— . . . .
If my grandparents were alive today—but they aren't— . . . .

4. The following sentences express conditions of *past speculation* (contrary to fact):

If she had applied for the management training program last year, she would have learned about financial planning. (But she didn't apply, so she didn't learn about financial planning.)

She wouldn't have paid her employees such high salaries if she had known about financial planning. (But she didn't know about financial planning, so she paid them too much.)

B. We can summarize the patterns of conditional verb tenses as shown in the box below. Some other forms can be used, and you will probably come across them in your reading. However, for the purpose of correctness in your own writing, use the box as a guide.

C. To practice using conditional forms, write a paragraph on each of these topics:

1. If you had $1 million, what would you do?
2. Tell a reader about something you once did that you wish you had not done. How would your life have been different if this had not happened?

CONDITIONAL SENTENCES

Meaning	If clause	Independent clause
Fact	Same tense in both (usually present)	
Future prediction	present	*will* *can* *should* *might* } + simple form
Present-future speculation	past *(were)*	*would* *could* etc. } + simple form
Past speculation	*had* + participle	*would have* *could have* etc. } + participle

3. Think of something that is likely to happen. Tell your reader what will happen as a result if this other event occurs.

D. Rewrite the following sentences, using a conditional clause with *if*:

1. I didn't see him, so I didn't pay him the money I owed him. (If I had seen him . . . .)
2. She doesn't spend much time with her children, so she doesn't know their friends.
3. He didn't lock the windows; a burglar climbed in and took his jewelry.
4. The woman wasn't able to find an ambulance, so her husband died on the street.
5. He doesn't have anyone to help him, so he won't finish the job on time.

(See Answer Key, p. 110.)

Editing Advice

If you have doubts about the accuracy of the tenses in a sentence with a conditional clause, ask the following questions:

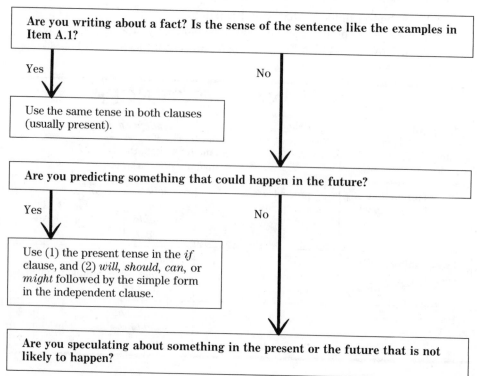

Are you writing about a fact? Is the sense of the sentence like the examples in Item A.1?

Yes

No

Use the same tense in both clauses (usually present).

Are you predicting something that could happen in the future?

Yes

No

Use (1) the present tense in the *if* clause, and (2) *will, should, can,* or *might* followed by the simple form in the independent clause.

Are you speculating about something in the present or the future that is not likely to happen?

(Flowchart continued)

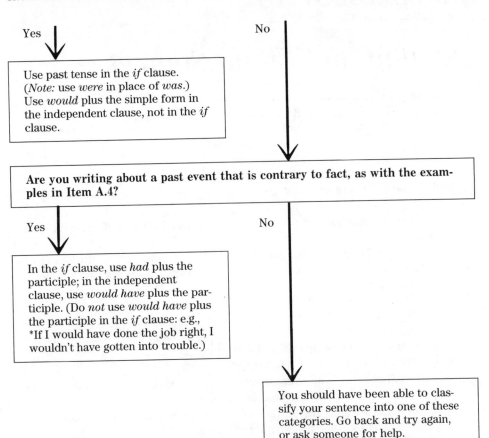

Yes ↓

Use past tense in the *if* clause.
(*Note:* use *were* in place of *was*.)
Use *would* plus the simple form in
the independent clause, not in the *if*
clause.

No ↓

Are you writing about a past event that is contrary to fact, as with the examples in Item A.4?

Yes ↓

In the *if* clause, use *had* plus the
participle; in the independent
clause, use *would have* plus the participle. (Do *not* use *would have* plus
the participle in the *if* clause: e.g.,
*If I would have done the job right, I
wouldn't have gotten into trouble.)

No ↓

You should have been able to clas-
sify your sentence into one of these
categories. Go back and try again,
or ask someone for help.

Quoting and Citing Sources

> *Question:* **When and how do I quote a speaker or writer?**

A. Look at the following passage:

> Mrs. Stein, with her hat on, came back into the room, digging into her purse.
>
> "Marilyn and I are going to that new Italian place," she said, "and I've lost the address. It's that real elegant place where they serve everything burning on a sword."
>
> Priscilla started coughing.
>
> "I think that cough is psychosomatic*," Lee said.
>
> Priscilla put a handkerchief to her lips, and Mrs. Stein said, "What does that mean? Does that mean we'll all get it?"
>
> "Probably," Lee said. "Probably."
>
> "Ah, here it is," the woman exclaimed, snatching a piece of paper from her purse. "Priscilla, don't light another cigarette."
>
> Priscilla was moving a hand around in the pocket of her mink coat.
>
> "What's this?" she asked, pulling out a small box. "Lee, it's for you."
>
> She handed him the box, which was from Tiffany's, and he opened it and found a pair of gold cuff links.

Write down answers to the following questions about the passage:

1. How are quotation marks and capital letters used with the following: (a) part of a sentence, (b) a complete sentence, and (c) more than one sentence?
2. What is the relative position of quotation marks and end-of-quotation punctuation?
3. What punctuation separates an introductory phrase like "He said" from a quotation?
4. When is a capital letter used to introduce a quotation—and when isn't one used?

*psychosomatic: caused by state of mind
Source: Aubrey Goodman, *The Golden Youth of Lee Prince*. Greenwich, Connecticut: Crest Books, 1959, p. 312.

5. With dialogue, when are new paragraphs formed?

(See Answer Key, p. 110.)

B. In the preceding passage, which is from a novel, direct quotation is used to record the exact words of a conversation. When you want to record dialogue directly, use direct quotation. You may also want to quote directly when you are writing an essay. Try to quote directly only passages that are particularly noteworthy, or do a great deal to support the point you want to make. You can quote whole sentences or parts of sentences.

Look carefully at the type of material quoted and at the punctuation and capitalization used with the quotation in these examples from journalism.

1. That can have important implications for the kids. "In general, the more question-asking the parents do, the higher the children's IQ's," Lewis says. (*Newsweek*, "The Analysts Who Came to Dinner")
2. Some men do help out, but for most husbands dinnertime remains a relaxing hour. While the female cooks and serves, Lewis says, "the male sits back and eats." (*Newsweek*, "The Analysts Who Came to Dinner")
3. Dr. Entin believes that pictures often say more than words because "people do not guard their body language with the same vigor as their words." (Jane E. Brody, "Photos Speak Volumes About Relationships")

How does the usage in these examples compare with the answers you gave to the questions in Item A?

C. Whenever you quote, you need to cite your source. That is, you need to tell your reader who said or wrote the words, where they appeared, and when. Sometimes, you might want to refer to an authority, but not quote exact words. In the following passage, the author does not quote directly but summarizes an expert's opinion on a controversial issue. However, the author still cites her source and lets us know where she found that opinion expressed:

In fact, based on interviews with hundreds of executives for her book *Paths to Power: A Woman's Guide From First Job to Top Executive* (Addison-Wesley, 1980), Ms. Josefowitz says that women are better managers than men. (Mary Schnack, "Are Women Bosses Better?")

Here the author tells us the title of the book, the author's name, the publisher, and the date of publication. When you write academic essays, you usually do not give all this information in the text of your essay, but at the end. You need to give your readers all the information they need to locate the source, including the exact page where you found the information.

Various disciplines have certain guidelines for citing sources. If you have to write a paper for a psychology course, for instance, make sure you ask your instructor what form to use. For essays in the humanities, for example, the Modern Language Association (MLA) recommends that you give a brief reference in parentheses in your text, so that your reader knows the author's name and the page number. Then, at the end of the essay, you include a list (alphabetical by author) of Works Cited, with full bibliographical details of each source.

The following example is a passage from an essay that cites two sources, a book and a magazine article.

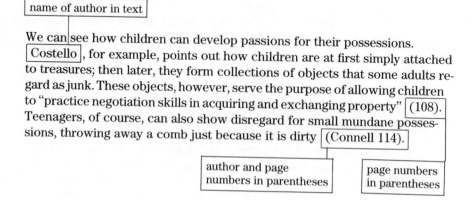

At the end of the essay, a list of Works Cited would appear, containing, in alphabetical order, the following two entries:

WORKS CITED

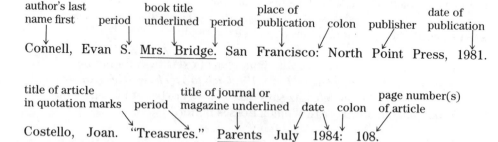

D. Read the passage from the article by Cherlin and Furstenberg that appears in Troublespot 8, Item C. In your own words, write a short summary of the ideas expressed in that excerpt. Include in it one direct quotation and note the page on which the excerpt appears in this book.

Editing Advice

If you have quoted directly in your piece of writing, ask these questions:

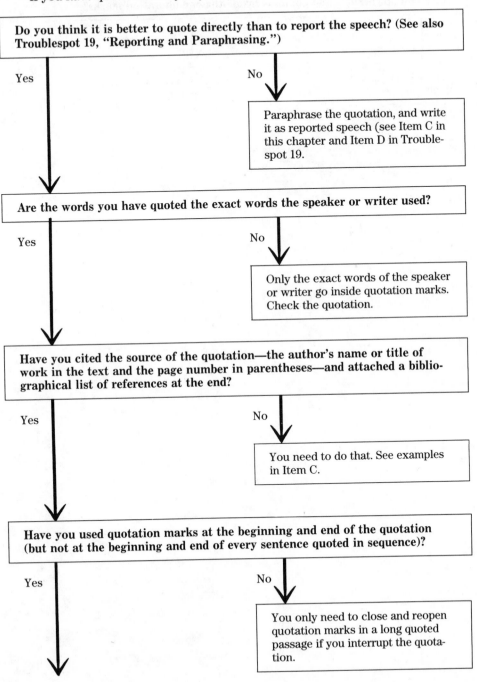

Do you think it is better to quote directly than to report the speech? (See also Troublespot 19, "Reporting and Paraphrasing.")

Yes

No

Paraphrase the quotation, and write it as reported speech (see Item C in this chapter and Item D in Troublespot 19.

Are the words you have quoted the exact words the speaker or writer used?

Yes

No

Only the exact words of the speaker or writer go inside quotation marks. Check the quotation.

Have you cited the source of the quotation—the author's name or title of work in the text and the page number in parentheses—and attached a bibliographical list of references at the end?

Yes

No

You need to do that. See examples in Item C.

Have you used quotation marks at the beginning and end of the quotation (but not at the beginning and end of every sentence quoted in sequence)?

Yes

No

You only need to close and reopen quotation marks in a long quoted passage if you interrupt the quotation.

(Flowchart continued)

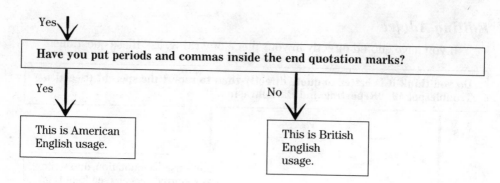

Yes

Have you put periods and commas inside the end quotation marks?

Yes   No

This is American
English usage.

This is British
English
usage.

Reporting and Paraphrasing

> **Question:** How is reporting what I hear or read different from quoting directly?

A. We use direct quotation when we are writing dialogue or when we are telling the reader exactly what somebody else said or wrote, word for word. We quote exact words when those words are particularly appropriate. If, however, we want to convey general ideas rather than exact words, we usually use reported speech. Note the difference in form:

The mayor asks, "How am I doing?"
The mayor asks how he is doing.

Here the introductory verb is in the present tense. With an introductory verb in the past, we would write this:

The mayor asked how he was doing.

Look closely at the two sentences below. Count the number of differences you can find between them.

The woman asked, "Where are my glasses?"
The woman asked where her glasses were.

(See Answer Key, p. 111.)

Sometimes, particularly when we report a long piece of speech or writing, it is better to paraphrase—that is, express in our own words the intention of the speaker or writer:

The mayor asked the people to assess his progress.
The woman wanted to find her glasses.

B. Look at the cartoon at the top of the next page. Write a description of each frame of the four-frame cartoon. First, quote directly what the characters Lucy and Charlie Brown say, using quotation marks. Begin like this:

© 1959 United Feature Syndicate, Inc.

One day Lucy was sitting and offering psychiatric help for five cents. Charlie Brown came along, sat down, and said, ". . . ."

(See Answer Key, p. 111.)

C. Now, rewrite your description of the cartoon. This time use reported speech. Keep the reported speech as close to the original quotations as possible. Observe the following conventions:

1. Do not use quotation marks.
2. Do not use a question mark at the end of a reported question.
3. In a reported question, use statement word order (subject + verb) and not question word order.
4. After an introductory verb in the past (like *said*), use past-tense verbs for the reported speech.
5. Pronouns like *I, we, you* change when you write reported speech.
6. *This* and *these* change to *that* and *those.*
7. Incomplete sentences usually have to be reworded slightly when they are reported.
8. Do not use the same introductory verb every time. Introductory verbs include *say, ask, tell someone to . . . , reply, complain, advise someone to . . . , want to know,* and others.

Begin like this:

One day Lucy was sitting and offering psychiatric help for five cents. Charlie Brown came along, sat down, and said that . . . .

(See Answer Key, p. 111.)

D. Usually, when we report speech, we do not simply transform the original words into reported speech. Instead, we tell about the ideas that were expressed, using our own words. That is, we paraphrase. A paraphrased report might look like this:

One day, when Lucy was offering psychiatric help for five cents, Charlie Brown visited her booth and complained of depression. He wanted advice on how to deal with it, but Lucy simply urged him not to be depressed—and charged him five cents anyway!

In an essay, always state where ideas come from. Even if you do not quote another writer exactly but just refer to and paraphrase his or her ideas, you still have to say where those ideas came from. You need to state the name of the author, the title of the work, the place and date of publication, and the publisher. You do this by mentioning the author or title and the page number (in parentheses) in your text and then giving the full bibliographic reference at the end of the paper. (See Item C in Troublespot 18 for examples.) Using another author's words or ideas as your own and not citing the source is *plagiarism*. This is *not acceptable* and could be illegal. For different methods of citing the sources of your ideas, consult your instructor or a handbook.

E. Look at the passage from *The Golden Youth of Lee Prince* on p. 80. With the book open in front of you, rewrite the passage, changing all the direct speech to reported speech. Use no direct quotation at all. Begin like this:

Mrs. Stein told the people in the room that she and Marilyn were going to a new Italian restaurant . . . .

(See Answer Key, p. 111.)

Now, close the book, and write another account of the conversation you have just rewritten. This time rely on your memory. Paraphrase the passage, and do not use any direct quotation. Concentrate on conveying the main gist of the conversation. The reporting does not have to be an exact sentence-by-sentence replica of the original.

Editing Advice

If you have written about what somebody else said or wrote, ask these questions:

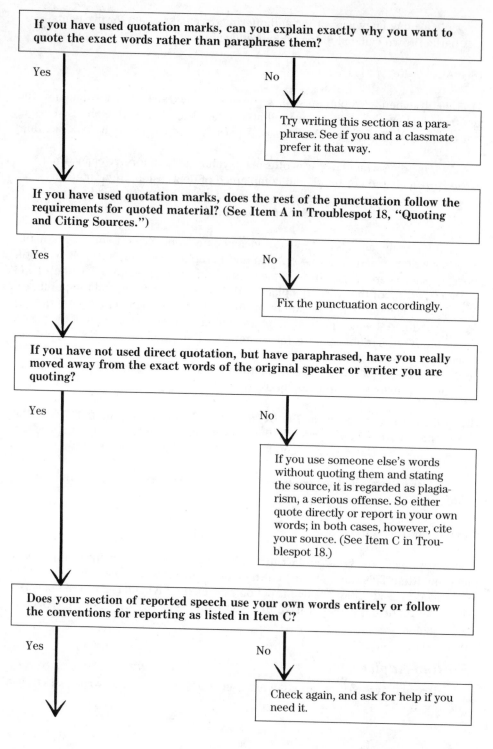

If you have used quotation marks, can you explain exactly why you want to quote the exact words rather than paraphrase them?

Yes   No

Try writing this section as a paraphrase. See if you and a classmate prefer it that way.

If you have used quotation marks, does the rest of the punctuation follow the requirements for quoted material? (See Item A in Troublespot 18, "Quoting and Citing Sources.")

Yes   No

Fix the punctuation accordingly.

If you have not used direct quotation, but have paraphrased, have you really moved away from the exact words of the original speaker or writer you are quoting?

Yes   No

If you use someone else's words without quoting them and stating the source, it is regarded as plagiarism, a serious offense. So either quote directly or report in your own words; in both cases, however, cite your source. (See Item C in Troublespot 18.)

Does your section of reported speech use your own words entirely or follow the conventions for reporting as listed in Item C?

Yes   No

Check again, and ask for help if you need it.

(Flowchart continued)

Yes

Now acknowledge the source of
your information briefly in the text
and then fully in a bibliographic reference at the end. (See Item D in
this chapter and Item C in Troublespot 18.)

TROUBLESPOT 20

Apostrophes for Possession

> *Question:* **How do I know whether to write *'s* or *-s'*?**

A. When we speak, *-'s* and *-s'* sound the same. But there is a difference in writing. Look at the following sentences:

1. a. The girl has a computer.	1. b. It is the girl's computer.
2. a. The girls have a computer.	2. b. It is the girls' computer.
3. a. The man has a computer.	3. b. It is the man's computer.
4. a. The men have a computer.	4. b. It is the men's computer.

What do you note about the four sentences labeled *b*? Why do you think sentence 2b looks different from the others? Write down an explanation. Look closely at the four sentences labeled *a* to help you find the answers. (See Answer Key, p. 111.)

B. Rewrite each of the following pairs of sentences as one sentence. Use an apostrophe to show possession. Make the italicized verb the verb of your new sentence. For example,

Their daughters took a vacation.
The vacation *was* wonderful.
New sentence: Their daughters' vacation was wonderful.

1. The baby has some toys.
   The toys *are* all over the floor.
2. The babies were crying.
   The crying *kept* everyone awake.
3. The house belongs to my family.
   The house *is* gigantic.
4. Ms. Johnson has a son.
   He *is* a lawyer.
5. The women have plans.
   Their plans *are* ambitious.
6. The politicians have plans.
   Their plans *are* ambitious.

(See Answer Key, p. 112.)

C. When you write two nouns together without an apostrophe and you want to check whether you need an apostrophe, see if you can reword the phrase using *of* or the idea of ownership:

*the girl computer = the computer of the girl *or,* the computer belonging to
                     the girl

This phrase needs an apostrophe to show possession: *the girl's computer.*
     If the idea of ownership does not work, as in *coffee shop,* you do not need an apostrophe. Also, if the first word of the two is the name of a building, an object, or a piece of furniture, you do not need an apostrophe: *hotel room, car door, table leg.*
     Note: The possessive adjective *its* shows possession but is *never* used with an apostrophe. (The form *it's* means "it is.")

The college announced *its* new policy.
It's [it is] a good policy.

D. Rewrite the following phrases, using an apostrophe. For example:

the bone belonging to the dog
·the dog's bone

     1. the room belonging to their daughters (i.e., two daughters share a room)
     2. the room belonging to their son (they have one son)
     3. the advice of the president
     4. the problems of the teachers
     5. the efforts of Ms. Johnson
     6. the toothbrush belonging to my brother
     7. the house belonging to his mother-in-law
     8. the decision made by my family

(See Answer Key, p. 112.)

Editing Advice

     If you have trouble deciding when and where to put an apostrophe to show possession, look carefully at any two nouns that are together in your piece of writing and ask these questions:

Is there an *of* or ownership relationship between the two nouns?

Yes ⬇   No ⬇

(Flowchart continued)

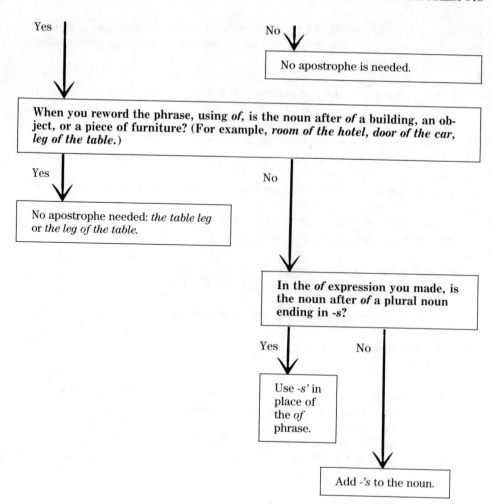

Yes

No

No apostrophe is needed.

When you reword the phrase, using *of,* is the noun after *of* a building, an object, or a piece of furniture? (For example, *room of the hotel, door of the car, leg of the table.*)

Yes

No apostrophe needed: *the table leg* or *the leg of the table.*

No

In the *of* expression you made, is the noun after *of* a plural noun ending in -*s*?

Yes

No

Use -*s'* in place of the *of* phrase.

Add -*'s* to the noun.

Commas

> *Question:* **What are the rules for using commas?**

A. It is more common to overuse commas than to omit them when they are needed. So, you might be able to use the rule "When in doubt, leave it out." However, there are several cases where the conventions are clear enough that there should be no doubt.

B. Commas are usually used in the following instances:

1. To set off a word, phrase, or clause before the subject of the sentence. (Some writers omit the comma if the introductory phrase is short.) For example:

   Wanting to impress all their friends, Jane and Jack Jones bought a Rolls-Royce.
   Because they wanted to impress their friends, Jane and Jack Jones bought a Rolls-Royce.
   In the spring of last year, Jane and Jack Jones bought a Rolls-Royce.
   Actually, they prefer to ride bicycles.

   but:

   Yesterday Jane and Jack bought a Rolls-Royce.

2. To separate items in a list:

   For the picnic, they packed *cheese, ham, egg salad, and roast beef.*
   The cabin in the woods has no *gas, electricity, or plumbing.*

3. To set off words, phrases, and clauses that are inserted as additional information at any position in the sentence. The reader does not need this information to understand the meaning of the independent clause. For example:

   Sally's boss, *a powerful individual,* refused to give her the day off.
   Sally's boss, *however,* refused to give her the day off.
   Sally's boss, *who had headed the company for fifteen years,* refused to give her the day off.

93

Sally's boss refused to give her any time off, *not even the day Sally had requested to attend her sister's wedding.*

You can think of these commas as a set of handles: they let you lift the enclosed words out of the sentence. After you do that, the reader will still be able to understand the sense of the independent clause: for example, "Sally's boss refused to give her the day off."

4. To set off a quotation:

F. Scott Fitzgerald said to his daughter, "Don't worry about anyone getting ahead of you."
"Don't worry about anyone getting ahead of you," F. Scott Fitzgerald said to his daughter.

5. To separate complete sentences joined by one of the seven connecting words *(and, but, or, nor, so, for, yet)*. In your reading, you might sometimes see the comma omitted. However, if you follow this convention and include the comma, it will not be considered wrong.

Her son is living in a small town in northern Oregon, and her two daughters have moved to Chicago.

Note: A comma is *not* used before a clause introduced by the subordinating word *that:*

It was astonishing that they made their business so successful.
He said that she should not worry.

C. Examine all the uses of commas in the sentences from Russell Baker's *Growing Up* that appear in Troublespot 6, Item F. Try to fit each comma use into one of the five categories in Item B of this chapter.

Example:

I was enjoying the luxuries of a rustic nineteenth century boyhood, but for the women Morrisonville life had few rewards.

Explanation:

The comma separates two complete sentences joined with *but.*

(See Answer Key, p. 112.)

Editing Advice

To make sure that every comma in your essay is necessary, examine each comma use and ask these questions:

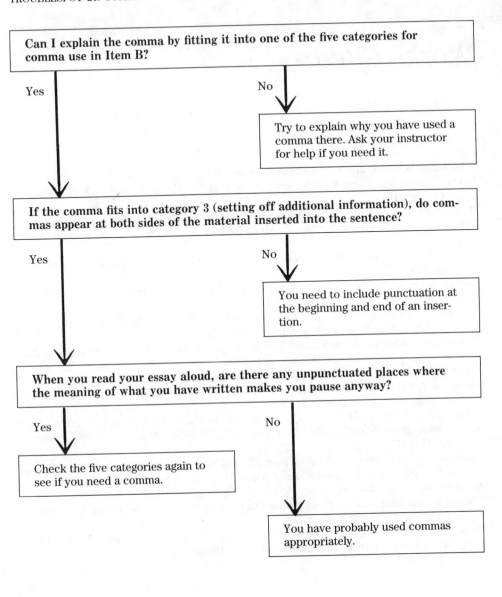

Can I explain the comma by fitting it into one of the five categories for comma use in Item B?

Yes

No

Try to explain why you have used a comma there. Ask your instructor for help if you need it.

If the comma fits into category 3 (setting off additional information), do commas appear at both sides of the material inserted into the sentence?

Yes

No

You need to include punctuation at the beginning and end of an insertion.

When you read your essay aloud, are there any unpunctuated places where the meaning of what you have written makes you pause anyway?

Yes

No

Check the five categories again to see if you need a comma.

You have probably used commas appropriately.

Works Cited

"The Analysts Who Came to Dinner." *Newsweek*, October 19, 1981, p. 92.

Baker, Russell. "The Paper Workingstuff." *Poor Russell's Almanac*. New York: Doubleday, 1972, pp. 151–153.

Baker, Russell. *Growing Up*. New York: Congdon and Weed, 1982, p. 43.

Brody, Jane E. "Photos Speak Volumes About Relationships." *The New York Times*, July 17, 1984, III, p. 1.

Cetron, Marvin J. "Getting Ready for the Jobs of the Future." *The Futurist*, June 1983, pp. 15 + .

Cherlin, Andrew, and Frank Furstenberg, Jr. "The American Family in the Year 2000." *The Futurist*, June 1983, pp. 7–10.

Connell, Evan S. *Mrs. Bridge*. San Francisco: North Point Press, 1981, p. 14.

Costello, Joan. "Treasures." *Parents*, July 1984, p. 108.

Csikszentmihalyi, Mihaly, and Eugene Rochberg-Halton. "Object Lessons." *Psychology Today*, December 1981, pp. 78–80 + .

Doherty, Jim. "Mr. Doherty Builds His Dream Life." *Money*, May 1982, pp. 77 + .

Goodman, Aubrey. *The Golden Youth of Lee Prince*. Greenwich, Connecticut: Crest Books, 1959, p. 312.

Johnson, Joyce. *Minor Characters*. Boston: Houghton Mifflin, 1983, p. 13.

Kagan, Julia. "Survey: Work in the 1980's and 1990's." *Working Woman*, July 1983, pp. 16–18.

Mays, Bruce. "In Fighting Trim." *New York Times Magazine*, September 2, 1984, p. 28.

Novak, William. "What Do Women Really Want?" *McCalls*, February 1983, pp. 10–12.

Schnack, Mary. "Are Women Bosses Better?" *McCalls*, August 1981, p. 39.

Stern, Barbara Lang. "Lure of Possessions: Do You Cling to Objects or Throw Away Your Past?" *Vogue*, March 1983, p. 173.

Toth, Susan Allen. *Blooming: A Small-Town Girlhood*. Boston: Little Brown, 1978, p. 125.

Toth, Susan Allen. *Ivy Days*. Boston: Little Brown, 1984, p. 156.

Appendix: Irregular Verbs

The -s and -ing forms of irregular verbs have been included only in instances where the spelling sometimes causes students trouble.

Simple Form	-s	-ing	Past	Participle
arise		arising	arose	arisen
be		being	was/were	been
beat		beating	beat	beaten
become		becoming	became	become
begin		beginning	began	begun
bend			bent	bent
bet		betting	bet	bet
bind			bound	bound
bite		biting	bit	bitten
bleed			bled	bled
blow			blew	blown
break			broke	broken
breed			bred	bred
bring			brought	brought
build			built	built
burst			burst	burst
buy			bought	bought
catch			caught	caught
choose		choosing	chose	chosen
cling			clung	clung
come		coming	came	come
cost	costs		cost	cost
creep		creeping	crept	crept
cut		cutting	cut	cut
deal			dealt	dealt
dig		digging	dug	dug
do	does		did	done
draw			drew	drawn
drink			drank	drunk
drive		driving	drove	driven
eat		eating	ate	eaten

Simple Form	-s	-ing	Past	Participle
fall			fell	fallen
feed			fed	fed
feel		feeling	felt	felt
fight			fought	fought
find			found	found
flee			fled	fled
fly	flies	flying	flew	flown
forbid		forbidding	forbad(e)/forbid	forbidden
forget		forgetting	forgot	forgotten
forgive		forgiving	forgave	forgiven
freeze		freezing	froze	frozen
get		getting	got	gotten/got (Brit.)
give		giving	gave	given
go			went	gone
grind			ground	ground
grow			grew	grown
hang*			hung	hung
have		having	had	had
hear			heard	heard
hide		hiding	hid	hidden
hit		hitting	hit	hit
hold			held	held
hurt			hurt	hurt
keep			kept	kept
know			knew	known
lay		laying	laid	laid
lead			led	led
leave		leaving	left	left
lend			lent	lent
let		letting	let	let
lie		lying	lay	lain
light			lit/lighted	lit/lighted
lose		losing	lost	lost
make		making	made	made
mean			meant	meant
meet		meeting	met	met
pay	pays		paid	paid
put		putting	put	put
quit		quitting	quit	quit
read		reading	read	read
ride		riding	rode	ridden
ring			rang	rung
rise		rising	rose	risen
run		running	ran	run

*(*Hang* in the sense of "put to death" is regular: *hang/hanged/hanged*)

Simple Form	-s	-ing	Past	Participle
say	says		said	said
see			saw	seen
seek			sought	sought
sell			sold	sold
send			sent	sent
set		setting	set	set
shake		shaking	shook	shaken
shine		shining	shone	shone
shoot			shot	shot
show			showed	shown/showed
shrink			shrank/shrunk	shrunk
shut		shutting	shut	shut
sing			sang	sung
sink			sank	sunk
sit		sitting	sat	sat
sleep		sleeping	slept	slept
slide		sliding	slid	slid
slit		slitting	slit	slit
speak			spoke	spoken
spend			spent	spent
spin		spinning	spun	spun
spit		spitting	spit	spit
split		splitting	split	split
spread			spread	spread
spring			sprang	sprung
stand			stood	stood
steal		stealing	stole	stolen
stick			stuck	stuck
sting			stung	stung
stink			stank	stunk
strike		striking	struck	struck
swear			swore	sworn
sweep		sweeping	swept	swept
swim		swimming	swam	swum
swing			swung	swung
take		taking	took	taken
teach			taught	taught
tear			tore	torn
tell			told	told
think			thought	thought
throw			threw	thrown
tread			trod	trod/trodden
understand			understood	understood
upset		upsetting	upset	upset
wake		waking	woke	waked/woken
wear			worn	worn

Simple Form	-s	-ing	Past	Participle
weave		weaving	wove	woven
weep		weeping	wept	wept
win		winning	won	won
wind			wound	wound
withdraw			withdrew	withdrawn
wring			wrung	wrung
write		writing	wrote	written

Answer Key

Note: There is often more than one correct answer to an exercise. If your answer is different from the answer here, do not assume your answer is wrong. You may have found an alternative solution. Check with your instructor.

Troublespot 1: Sentence Structure and Boundaries

A. Standard Sentences in Written English

Note: There are more possibilities than those given here. If you have other versions, check them with your instructor.

1. The sun came out.
2. OK
3. The beach looked lovely. [Punctuation needed at end.]
4. The waves were splashing on the sand. *or* The beach looked lovely, with the waves splashing on the sand.
5. We were playing games. *or* We played games.
6. We ate our picnic. *or* We played games and ate our picnic.
7. We ate ham sandwiches.
8. OK
9. We were having such a good time. *or* Because we were having such a good time, we stayed there for four hours, sunbathing and swimming.

B. Correcting Sentence Fragments

1. Fragment: A great big black one.
   The little girl saw a spider, a great big black one. *or* The little girl saw a great big black spider.
2. Fragment: To try to scare the spider.
   She screamed loudly to try to scare the spider.
3. Fragment: Because she was frightened.
   Because she was frightened, she ran into another room.
4. Fragment: Her legs still shaking.
   Her legs were still shaking. *or* She sat down next to her mother, her legs still shaking.

Troublespot 2: Combining Sentences: Coordinating

D. Linking Expressions

for example: provides an example of how passions develop
then later: shows sequence of events
however: points out a contrast between how adults regard collections and how collections function for children
of course: emphasizes the fact that teenagers (as opposed to younger children) do not always treasure objects
also: adds the idea that teenagers can show disregard for small possessions

E. Connecting Sentences

Only one of the possibilities for each pair is listed:
1. . . . ; for instance, he always wrote standing up.
2. . . . ; in addition, he was an active sportsman.
3. . . . . However, he shifted to his typewriter when the writing was easy for him. . . .
4. . . . . He was, nevertheless, a neat person at heart.
5. . . . ; in fact, he hardly ever threw anything away.
6. . . . ; for example, he wrote the ending to *A Farewell to Arms* thirty-nine times.
7. . . . . Then, after lunch, . . .
8. . . . . As a result, his landlady worried that he wasn't eating enough.

F. Using Connecting Words or Linking Expressions

His parents took him to the United States in 1946. The family spoke. . . .
Now my grandfather no longer speaks Polish or German at home; he speaks only English.
His children don't speak Polish at all. However, they understand it a little.

Troublespot 3: Combining Sentences: Subordinating

D. Combining Sentences

Here are a few of the possibilities:
Since Jack, our administrative assistant, wanted to make a good impression, he wore his brother's new suit, the pants of which kept falling down because the suit was big for him.
To make a good impression, Jack, our administrative assistant, wore his brother's new suit, but the pants kept falling down because the suit was big for him.
Although our administrative assistant, Jack, wore a new suit belonging to his brother in order to make a good impression, the suit was too big for him, so the pants kept falling down.

E. Combined Sentences

1. There are two independent clauses: *Jack wore his brother's new suit.* and *The suit was so big for him.*
2. Subject + verb = *Jack wore* and *the suit was*
3. The independent clauses are connected by *but.*
4. There is one subordinate clause: *that the pants kept falling down* (result).
5. Other attachments are condensed phrases: *wanting to make a good impression, our administrative assistant.*

F. Separating Sentences

Her picture is in a heavy silver frame.
The frame is of ornate primitive design.
The frame was brought by my uncle from Peru.
The picture shows her as a young woman.
The picture is placed on the polished lid [of the piano].
The lid is never opened.
The piano tuner comes and opens it.

G. Combining Sentences

Only one or two possibilities for each group of sentences is given below. There are others. Check with your instructor to find out if yours is accurate:

1. As I watched a little girl carrying a big shopping bag, I felt so sorry for her that I offered to help.
2. When my huge family met at my grandparents' house every holiday, there were never enough chairs, so I always had to sit on the floor.
3. Computers save so much time that many businesses are buying them, but the managers sometimes don't realize that they have to train people to operate the machines.
4. All their lives they have lived with their father, a powerful politician who has made lots of enemies.
5. Wanting to be successful, she worked day and night for a famous advertising agency until eventually she became a vice-president.
6. Although he really wants to go skiing, he has decided to go to a beach resort in California since his sister, who(m) he hasn't seen for 10 years, lives there. *or* Although he really wants to go skiing, he has decided to go to a beach resort in California to visit his sister, whom he hasn't seen for 10 years.

Troublespot 5: Negatives

F. Verb Forms with *Neither . . . Nor*

The verb agrees with the last item of the pair in the *neither . . . nor* subject:
the children have (plural subject—plural verb form: no *-s*)
the mother has (singular subject—singular verb form: *-s*)

G. Alternative Forms of Negation

Workaholics have no time for their family. They think nothing is as important as their job
. . . . Workaholics can never really relax . . . . They won't go anywhere unless . . . .
Often, on a weekend away, workaholics won't talk to anybody . . . .

Troublespot 6: Nouns

F. Identify and Categorize Nouns

1. luxuries: common/countable/plural
   boyhood: common/countable/singular
   women: common/countable/plural
   life: common/uncountable
   rewards: common/countable/plural
2. mother: common/countable/singular
   grandmother: common/countable/singular
   house: common/uncountable (idiom = to keep house)
   women: common/countable/plural
   Civil War: proper
3. electricity: common/uncountable
   gas: common/uncountable
   plumbing: common/uncountable
   heating: common/uncountable
4. baths: common/countable/plural
   laundry: common/uncountable
   dishwashing: common/uncountable
   buckets: common/countable/plural
   water: common/uncountable
   spring: common/countable/singular
   foot: common/countable/singular
   hill: common/countable/singular
5. floors: common/countable/plural
   hands: common/countable/plural
   knees: common/countable/plural
   rugs: common/countable/plural
   carpet beaters: common/countable/plural
   chickens: common/countable/plural
   bread: common/uncountable
   pastries: common/countable/plural
   clothing: common/uncountable
   sewing machines: common/countable/plural
6. end: common/countable/singular
   day: common/countable/singular
   woman: common/countable/singular
   serf: common/countable/singular
7. [men]: common/countable/plural
   basins: common/countable/plural

      supper: common/uncountable
      porch: common/countable/singular
      night: common/countable/singular
8. women: common/countable/plural
      twilight: common/uncountable (used here as adjective)
      music: common/uncountable
      Morrisonville: proper

G. Mistakes with Noun Capitals and Plurals

Corrections of errors:
suitcase: suitcases
all the store: all the stores
Town: town
three dress: three dresses
spain: Spain

Troublespot 7: Verb Tenses

C. Switch in Time Zone

The writer signaled the switch in time zone with the word *once*, telling us that she was going to describe an event in the past.

D. Identify Verb Phrase, Time Zone, Time Relationship, and Signal

love: Present/simple present
watch: Present/simple present
can get: Present/simple present
was: Past/simple past (signal: three months ago)
spent: Past/simple past
will be: Future/simple future (signal: three months from now)
will be cultivating . . . , weeding . . . killing: Future/in progress at a known time in the
      future
had to reshingle: Past/simple past (signal: recently)
will help: Future/simple future (signal: soon)
supplements: Present/simple present
are working: Present/in progress at a known time in the present
will spray . . . , paint . . . , plant . . . clean: Future/simple future (signal: later this month)
arrive: Future/simple present (in time clause)

Troublespot 8: Verb Forms

C. Underline Complete Verb Phrase

1. had divorced, hadn't seen, had managed (to see), persists, will spend, reach, has been written, has (not yet) proven, occur, does occur, head, experience, do (not) experience
2. is made, are made, is repaired, make, make, will fall apart, will be, is encouraged (to throw away and buy), are making

Troublespot 9: Agreement

B. Identify Verbs

- The verbs are: pursues, oversees, bakes, cans, freezes, chauffeurs, practices, takes, does, writes, tends, stacks, delivers
- With a plural subject ("Sandy and her sister") all these verbs will change to the "no -s" form: *pursue, oversee*, etc.
- Other changes:
  her: their
  she: they
  herself: themselves

F. Determine Whether "There Is" or "There Are" Is Correct

1. There are, 2. There is, 3. There is, 4. There is, 5. There are, 6. There is, 7. There are, 8. There are, 9. There is, 10. There are.

Troublespot 10: Active and Passive

E. Determine Active and Passive Verbs

1. consider: active
   is being made: passive
   is being repaired: passive
   will be discarded: passive
   wears out: active
   will be set: passive
2. will forget: active
   were buried: passive
3. is: active
   will occur: active
   are going to affect: active
   work: active
   are educated: passive
   (are) trained: passive
   is: active
   will retire: active
   was forced: passive
   will be filling: active

Troublespot 11: Pronouns

C. Answers to Specific Questions (e.g., What does *this* refer to?)

1. beauty, originality, and skills
2. the one just described, with the run-over heels, etc.
3. the one before
4. the fact that women hold so few management positions

D. Personal Pronouns/Demonstratives and People/Objects They Refer To

it: a blanket or toy animal
they: most children
they: most children
its: the object's (referent is *object*)
their: children's (referent is *children*)
they: children
they: children
them: children
these things: certain objects

Troublespot 12: Articles

E. Articles and Determiners with Nouns and Their Special Categories

families: countable/plural/nonspecific
their members: countable/plural/possessive adjective (specific)
a lot of support: uncountable/quantity word (nonspecific)
a child: countable/singular/nonspecific
a child: countable/singular/nonspecific
a fight: countable/singular/nonspecific
a friend: countable/singular/nonspecific
the child's mother: countable/singular/possessive noun (specific)
home: idiom: at home
an aunt: countable/singular/nonspecific
a grandmother: countable/singular/nonspecific
advice: uncountable/nonspecific
six years: countable/plural/numeral (nonspecific)
my bicycle: countable/singular/possessive adjective (specific)
the block: countable/singular/specific
a race: countable/singular/nonspecific
my friends: countable/plural/possessive adjective (specific)
my father: countable/singular/possessive adjective (specific)
my mother: countable/singular/possessive adjective (specific)
the house: countable/singular/specific
people: countable (one person, two people)/plural/nonspecific
my aunt: countable/singular/possessive adjective (specific)
my knees: countable/plural/possessive adjective (specific)
my grandmother: countable/singular/possessive adjective (specific)
a glass: countable/singular/nonspecific
milk: uncountable/nonspecific
a cookie: countable/singular/nonspecific
my uncle: countable/singular/possessive adjective (specific)
the doctor's office: countable/singular/possessive noun (specific)

Troublespot 13: Adjectives

F. Categories in Noun Phrases

1. that: determiner
   sophisticated: opinion
   young: age
   Italian: nationality
   model: head noun
2. his: determiner
   comfortable: opinion
   white: color
   velvet: material
   couch: head noun
3. two: determiner
   middle-aged: age
   Catholic: religion
   bishops: head noun
4. their: determiner
   charming: opinion
   little: size
   wood: material
   cabin: head noun

G. Categories in Noun Phrases

1. table: noun
2. plastic: material
3. a: determiner
   little: size
   silver: material
4. a: determiner
   French: nationality
5. a: determiner
   little: size
   tin: material
6. a: determiner
   circular: shape
   straw: material
   place: noun
7. three: determiner
   buffalo: noun
8. an: determiner
   ancient: age
   ivory: material

Troublespot 14: Adverbs

C. Adverbial Forms

happily, simply, carefully, successfully, fortunately, basically, angrily, possibly

Troublespot 15: -ing and Participle Forms

D. Examples of Some of the Possibilities

• Past tense form:
  The loud radio *annoyed* Julie as she lay on the beach in the sun.
• *-ing* form:
  Julie found the radio *annoying.*
  The loud radio was *annoying* to Julie.
  The loud radio was so *annoying* that Julie left the beach.
• Participle form:
  Annoyed by the loud radio, Julie left the beach.
  Julie was so *annoyed* by the loud radio that she left the beach.

E. *"-Ing"* Forms or the Participle Form

1. saving, getting rid, marking
2. collecting, fishing, enjoying, found, looking
3. constructed, discarded, set
4. forced, filling, displaced
5. surprised, disappointed

F. Combine Sentences with *"-ing"* or a Participle

1. Wanting to get the job, she arrived early for the interview.
2. The gray-haired man wearing a blue coat is my father.
3. We saw an exciting movie last week.
4. Confused by the examination questions, the student failed the exam.
5. The painting stolen from the museum yesterday was extremely valuable.
6. Asked to share his toys, the little boy screamed and cried. *or* When asked to . . . , . . .
7. She twisted her ankle (while) playing in the tennis tournament.

Troublespot 16: Relative Clauses

G. Combine Sentences with Relative Clause

Only one method of combining is given here. Others are possible. Check with your instructor.
1. The man who won the race was awarded a prize.
2. The girl who is sitting in the front row asks a lot of questions.
3. The people [that] I met at a party last night are from California.
4. The house [that] he is living in is gigantic.

5. Ms. McHam, who lives next door to me, is a lawyer. [This clause has commas around it.]
6. The journalist whose story you read yesterday has won a lot of prizes.
7. The radio [that] I bought was made in Taiwan.
8. She told her friends about the book [that] she had just read.
9. The man whose dog I am looking after is a radio announcer.

H. Combine Sentences with Relative Clause

1. At the lecture there were thirty-three people, most of whom lived in the neighborhood.
2. They waited half an hour for the committee members, some of whom just did not show up.
3. I sang three songs, one of which was "Singing in the Rain."
4. The statewide poetry competition was held last month, and she submitted four poems, none of which won a prize.
5. On every wall of his house he has hundreds of books, most of which are detective novels.

Troublespot 17: Conditions

D. Rewrite with Conditional Clause

1. If I had seen him, I would have paid him the money I owed him.
2. If she spent more time with her children, she would know their friends.
3. If he had locked the windows, a burglar would not have climbed in and taken his jewelry.
4. If the woman had been able to find an ambulance, her husband wouldn't have died on the street.
5. If he had someone to help him, he would finish the job on time.

Troublespot 18: Quoting and Citing Sources

A. Answers to Questions

1. a. When part of a sentence is quoted, the part does not begin with a capital letter: "and I've lost the address . . . ."
b. When a whole sentence is quoted, it begins with a capital letter, begins and ends with quotation marks, and the quotation marks come after the punctuation that signals the end of the quotation: "What's this?" she asked. A quoted complete sentence that does not appear at the end of the written sentence ends in a comma, not a period: "Ah, here it is," the woman exclaimed.
c. When more than one sentence is quoted, quotation marks do not appear at the beginning and end of every sentence, but only at the beginning and end of the passage quoted: Mrs. Stein said, "What does that mean? Does that mean we'll all get it?"

2. Quotation marks regularly come after the end-of-quotation punctuation: "Marilyn and I are going to that new Italian place," she said.

3. A comma: Mrs. Stein said, "What does that mean? . . ."

4. A capital letter is used when a complete sentence is quoted. If the quotation begins in the middle of a sentence, no capital letter is used: "Marilyn and I are going to that new Italian place," she said, "and I've lost the address . . . ."

5. A new paragraph marks a change of speaker.

Troublespot 19: Reporting and Paraphrasing

A. Determine the Differences in the Sentences

There are seven differences: no comma, no capital letter for *where*, no quotation marks, *are/were*, *my/her*, statement word order, no question mark.

B. Quote Directly

One version follows: Charlie Brown came along, sat down, and said, "I have deep feelings of depression." Then he asked, "What can I do about this?" Lucy replied, "Snap out of it! Five cents please."

C. Change to Reported Speech

One version follows, providing an example of a reported statement, question, and command: Charlie Brown came along, sat down, and said that he had deep feelings of depression. He asked Lucy what he could do about that. She advised him to snap out of it and politely asked him for five cents.

E. Change to Reported Speech

One version follows. Others are possible.

Mrs. Stein told the people in the room that she and Marilyn were going to a new Italian restaurant, an elegant place where they served everything burning on a sword. However, she had lost the address. At that point, Priscilla started coughing, and Lee wondered aloud if the cough was psychosomatic. Mrs. Stein didn't know what that word meant and wanted to know if they would all get the cough. Lee said they probably would. Suddenly, Mrs. Stein found the piece of paper with the address on it. As Priscilla put her hand in her mink-coat pocket, Mrs. Stein told her not to light another cigarette, but Priscilla pulled out a little box and told Lee it was for him. It was a Tiffany's box, and in it he found a pair of gold cuff links.

Troublespot 20: Apostrophes for Possession

A. Answers to Questions

All four sentences include an apostrophe.
Sentence 2b has the apostrophe after the final -*s*.

Sentence 2b has the apostrophe after the -*s* because the word *girls* already ends in -*s*. None of the other nouns (*girl, man, men*) end in -*s*.

B. Rewrite with Apostrophes

1. The baby's toys are all over the floor.
2. The babies' crying kept everyone awake.
3. My family's house is gigantic.
4. Ms. Johnson's son is a lawyer.
5. The women's plans are ambitious.
6. The politicians' plans are ambitious.

D. Rewrite with Apostrophes

1. their daughters' room
2. their son's room
3. the president's advice
4. the teachers' problems
5. Ms. Johnson's efforts
6. my brother's toothbrush
7. his mother-in-law's house
8. my family's decision

Troublespot 21: Commas

C. Fit Commas into Categories

They had no electricity, gas, plumbing, or central heating. The commas separate items in a list.

For baths, laundry, and dishwashing, they hauled buckets of water . . . The first two commas separate items in a list. The third comma sets off a prepositional phrase before the subject of the sentence.

They scrubbed floors on hands and knees, thrashed rugs . . . All the commas in this sentence separate items in a list. The list is a list of verbs: *scrubbed, thrashed,* etc.

. . . and, when supper was eaten, climbed up onto . . . The commas set off a clause of time that is inserted as additional information in to the middle of *The men scrubbed themselves and climbed . . .*

Presently the women joined them, and the twilight music of Morrisonville began. The comma separates two complete sentences joined with *and*.

Index